FOR THE LOVE OF
THE NAVY

A COMPANION

RAY HAMILTON

summersdale

FOR THE LOVE OF THE NAVY

Summersdale Publishers Ltd
46 West Street
Chichester
West Sussex
PO19 1RP
UK

www.summersdale.com

Printed and bound in the Czech Republic

ISBN: 978-1-78685-064-5

Substantial discounts on bulk quantities of Summersdale books are available to corporations, professional associations and other organisations. For details contact general enquiries: telephone: +44 (0) 1243 771107 or email: enquiries@summersdale.com.

CONTENTS

ACKNOWLEDGEMENTS

My thanks first and foremost to Cdre Dick Twitchen, CBE, a destroyer man and former Commodore Portsmouth Flotilla, for his expert advice and good humour throughout, and for showing me around the Portsmouth Naval Base, the highlight of which was an afternoon spent on board the destroyer HMS *Dragon*. I was privileged that afternoon to enjoy the hospitality of Captain Craig Wood, who modestly described himself as the 'driver' of that magnificent vessel and who took the time and trouble to give me a full guided tour during final preparations for putting to sea the next day. The members of the ship's company I was fortunate to meet or observe on board *Dragon* that afternoon exuded professionalism coupled with an obvious joy in what they were doing. We should be grateful to them, and to all who serve in the Royal Navy and Royal Marines, for protecting the interests of the nation while we carry on largely oblivious to their efforts on our behalf.

I am grateful also to Admiral Sir Jonathon Band, former First Sea Lord of the Naval Service, who not only took the time and trouble to read through my manuscript, but was also kind enough to provide the Foreword to the book having done so.

Thanks as always to Summersdale Publishers, especially Claire Plimmer for the opportunity to write once more about one of my great interests in life; Debbie Chapman for her expert management on this, our fourth collaboration; and Chris Turton for his always sound editing and advice. I am grateful also to Madeleine Stevens for rendering the manuscript shipshape with a professional and thorough copy-edit, and to Sarah Herman for an excellent final proofread in which she involved her father, Commander Tom Herman OBE Royal Navy, a former submarine commander who spent a total of fifty years in the Navy, and who is now a Friend of the Royal Navy Submarine Museum. His comments were an unexpected bonus that enabled me to be as technically correct as possible when referring to the intriguing world of the Submarine Service.

FOREWORD

BY ADMIRAL SIR JONATHON BAND, GCB, DL
FIRST SEA LORD, 2006–09

From the time I joined the Navy in 1967, I knew there was nowhere I would rather forge a career, be it as a junior officer on board ship, through the honour of sea command to Commander-in-Chief Fleet. As First Sea Lord, I pushed strongly for the modern, capable Navy that we have today.

The Navy, of course, has been at the heart of world history for a lot longer than my years in service and in this book Ray Hamilton encapsulates many of the events, ships and people that have made it such a fascinating and esteemed institution. The technology in the days of 'wooden ships and iron men' may seem dated in this information age but the advances made were significant and provided the edge needed in combat. The book highlights the major developments that took the Navy from the age of sail through steam and on into the capabilities of today's fleet. In addition, the changing face of shipboard life has not been neglected.

It is the people who are the beating heart of the Navy and its greatest single factor; operating in an unforgiving environment at sea that, in common with all mariners, sets them apart from others. In today's world they are seldom seen at work, whether below or above the waves and often beyond the horizon in a grey ship on a grey sea on a grey day, but their deeds are the bedrock of a nation's admiration for the Senior Service.

INTRODUCTION

This book is a celebration of the British Navy, which became the greatest single influence on world affairs for hundreds of years, and which remains today at the cutting edge of the advanced technology required to protect a nation's interests at home and abroad. We will start with a whistle-stop tour of its magnificent history, marvelling at famous ships and battles along the way. We will pay homage to the people who have chosen a life less ordinary to serve in its ranks, consider the many technological breakthroughs, and look at the organisation, roles and responsibilities of today's ultra-modern force.

Our naval history has its humble origins in the oar-driven victories achieved by Saxon kings Alfred and Athelstan against the Vikings in the ninth and tenth centuries, but really got going with Henry VIII. Our first great 'sea king' deployed an entire fleet of sail-driven, line-of-battle ships that could pound away with naval gunnery until the enemy had been defeated. The Elizabethan Navy of his daughter followed up by building the beginnings of a worldwide empire and by seeing off the Spanish Armada.

The Royal Navy as the institution we know and love today came into being in 1660 upon the restoration of the monarchy. The Corps of the Royal Marines, the other major component of Her Majesty's Naval Service to this day, can trace its roots back to 1664. Together, they have been punching above the weight of a tiny island nation ever since.

Our Navy rose to become the world's dominant naval power and enjoyed remarkable success in the French Revolutionary and Napoleonic Wars, which effectively ended all competition to rule the waves for the next hundred years, during which time the Navy took on the role of international policeman, starting with the longest campaign in its history – to bring about the abolition of slavery. As wood and sail gave way to steel and steam, the Royal Navy embraced the new technology faster than anyone else to herald in the era of the dreadnought.

Even after its important contributions to victory in two world wars, the Navy refused to rest on its laurels, playing its part in modern times to safeguard the seas and restore peace where necessary across the globe. The modern roles and responsibilities of a high-technology navy include conflict prevention, counterterrorism, anti-piracy, counternarcotics and humanitarian and disaster relief, all areas in which the Navy has developed major expertise.

The awe-inspiring vessels we will look at range from the Tudor warship *Mary Rose* to the brand-new aircraft carrier HMS *Queen Elizabeth*, the largest warship ever built for the Navy. We will pay due attention as we go to the likes of Nelson's flagship HMS *Victory*, the first steam-powered warship HMS *Warrior*, the revolutionary battleship HMS *Dreadnought*, the ill-fated 'Mighty Hood' and the most successful British battleship of all time, HMS *Warspite*. We will also look at the capabilities and impact of the first nuclear submarines.

The sea battles highlighted within the book include the Battle of Gravelines, which staved off the Spanish Armada; the Battle of Quiberon Bay, which put paid to French hopes of invading Britain during the Seven Years' War; the Glorious First of June and the Battle of the Nile, the two most significant victories of the French Revolutionary Wars; the Battle of Trafalgar, a major turning point in the Napoleonic Wars; the Battle of Jutland, the greatest naval conflict of World War One; the Battle of the Atlantic, fought to keep our supply lines open throughout World War Two; and the Falklands Conflict of 1982, following Argentina's invasion of those islands.

We will also look at the air capabilities of the Navy, from the time when HMS *Pallas* deployed kites to spread anti-Napoleonic leaflets across France to the state-of-the-art helicopters of today and the introduction of the F-35B Lightning II stealth jets that are very much a part of the future of the Fleet Air Arm (FAA).

As naval technology has moved on somewhat from the days of cannon fire, we will consider as we go the developments that have ultimately led us to the age of satellite technology, nuclear power and unmanned warriors.

The Navy is nothing without the men and women who serve within its ranks, though, from its highly trained sailors, aircrews and marine commandos to those who provide essential support at sea or on dry land. We will consider their roles and contributions throughout history, alongside their unique culture and traditions. We will look at what life afloat (or submerged) truly means and at the mystical Navy language known historically as 'Jackspeak'. If you have ever wondered about the origins of everyday expressions like 'toeing the line' or wanting a 'square meal' served 'piping hot', you will soon wonder no more.

A NOTE TO READERS

One of the many unique traditions of the Royal Navy is that shore establishments are referred to as 'stone frigates' and are named 'HMS (His or Her Majesty's Ship) something or other', just as if they were real ships (the background to which is explained in the 'Navy Traditions' chapter of the book). For the benefit of readers who are unfamiliar with the dark arts of naval nomenclature, I have therefore distinguished between real ships and stone frigates within this book as follows:

The names of ships and submarines are italicised, as is the long-standing worldwide convention in such matters, e.g. HMS *Victory*.

The names of stone frigates are not italicised, e.g. HMS Collingwood (the parent establishment of the Maritime Warfare School in Hampshire).

PART ONE

A BRIEF HISTORY OF THE NAVY

The Royal Navy of England hath ever been its greatest defence and ornament; it is its ancient and natural strength – the floating bulwark of our island.

WILLIAM BLACKSTONE

THE EARLY HISTORY
OF THE NAVY
(UP TO 1660)

The Navy is very old and very wise.

RUDYARD KIPLING

Although there was no permanent standing navy of any great significance anywhere in Britain until Henry VIII got England's seafaring act together in the sixteenth century, English and Scottish kings had been dabbling in naval warfare for up to a thousand years before that. We will start with a potted history of those early days before considering the might of the Tudor Navy and the way in which the Navy moved up a gear during the period of the Commonwealth that followed the English Civil War.

THE BEGINNINGS OF NAVAL
WARFARE IN BRITAIN

Seventh century: The fact that an Anglo-Saxon warrior king was buried inside a ship at Sutton Hoo in East Anglia suggests that naval warfare was already happening around the coastline of Britain at that time.

851:        King Athelstan of Wessex won a victory against the Vikings at Sandwich, Kent, capturing nine Viking ships in the process.

896:        King Alfred had nine longships built and with them he inflicted a further defeat on the Vikings when he trapped six of their ships off the south coast of England.

1008:   King Ethelred the Unready ordered the construction of a national fleet but couldn't command the loyalty of his commanders and failed with a raid against Norway.

1016:   King Canute had a standing navy of sixteen ships built but Edward the Confessor stood it back down in 1050.

1054:   Earl Siward of Northumbria sailed north on behalf of Edward the Confessor to defeat the Scottish ruler Macbeth, thereby earning himself a mention in Shakespeare's 'Scottish play' over half a century later.

1155:   With a regular need for secure cross-Channel travel between his lands in Britain and France, Henry II raised a naval force by commissioning the Cinque Ports of Hastings, New Romney, Hythe, Dover and Sandwich to provide him with the ships he needed.

1217:   An English fleet secured an important victory over French invaders at the Battle of Sandwich, cutting off supplies and reinforcements to Louis VIII and forcing him to abandon his occupation of London, thereby leaving the nine-year-old King Henry III to get on with the business of ruling England under the guidance of his self-appointed advisers.

1315–18: After Robert the Bruce had secured Scottish independence from England following the Battle of Bannockburn in 1314, he built the Royal Scots Navy, which he used to bring the Lords of the Isles into line and unsuccessfully invade Ireland.

1337–1453: During the Hundred Years' War with France, the English Navy initially consisted of commandeered merchant vessels, which were increasingly withdrawn by the merchants after successive kings refused to honour payments to them and even taxed them for using the 'King's ships' for reasons of commerce in between naval engagements. Henry V finally got the message and built his own fleet between 1413 and 1418. Notwithstanding this inconsistent approach to funding the Navy, the English won some significant naval battles during the war.

GREAT SEA BATTLES
TWO NAVAL ENGAGEMENTS OF THE HUNDRED YEARS' WAR

THE BATTLE OF SLUYS (1340)

Edward III and his son, the Black Prince, sailed into the inlet between West Flanders and Zeeland and obliterated the larger navy of Philip IV of France. The French ships had no answer to the efficient longbows of the English archers or the men-at-arms who subsequently boarded their vessels once the arrows had finally stopped raining down on them.

THE BATTLE OF WINCHELSEA (1350)

Also known as the Battle of *les Espagnols sur Mer* ('Spaniards on the Sea'), this was the first major battle to be fought by an English fleet in the open sea, just off the south-east coast of England. Once more, Edward III and his son, the Black Prince, upset the odds by defeating a joint Castilian and Genoese pirate force that had much larger and higher ships. Archery was again the order of the day, with English longbows pitched against the crossbows of the enemy, following which grappling irons were used to draw in and board enemy ships for the inevitable and gruesome hand-to-hand fighting that always brought an end to sea battles at that time.

1418:   Towards the end of Henry V's shipbuilding programme, which had increased the size of the Navy from six to thirty-nine ships over a five-year period, he launched his impressive-looking flagship *Grace Dieu*, but her service to the Navy was to prove somewhat ignominious.

FAMOUS SHIPS

Grace Dieu

Comparable in size to the future HMS *Victory*, and one of the largest ships of her time, the high-sided *Grace Dieu* needed 2,735 oak, 1,145 beech and fourteen ash trees and a specially built dock in Southampton for her construction. She sailed just once, but only after a mutiny before leaving port, because the crew objected to having soldiers and archers on board to guard against attack. After a further mutiny once under sail, the captain brought the ship into port on the Isle of Wight, where the crew made off. Subsequently laid up in the River Hamble, she was set on fire by a bolt of lightning in 1439. What remained below the waterline sank to the bottom, where she lies to this day.

THE TUDOR NAVY (1485–1603)

As ships began to have cannons mounted for the first time, Henry VII embarked on his own shipbuilding programme and had a dry dock built in Portsmouth for that purpose. Much of the funding for Henry VIII's subsequent expansion of the fleet came from his plundering of the monasteries following his break with the Catholic Church. The Elizabethan Navy of Henry VIII's daughter, Elizabeth I, made its own place in naval history by defeating the Spanish Armada.

1512:   Henry VIII's flagship *Henri Grace à Dieu*, aka *Great Harry*, was built to outdo the largest warship in Europe at the time, the *Great Michael*, which had been launched by the Royal Scots Navy the year before.

1545:   The French arrived with 200 ships and 30,000 fighting men to invade England, but were so utterly incompetent that the eighty ships and 12,000 men of the English Navy easily saw them off at the two-day Battle of the Solent, today remembered mostly for the sinking of the *Mary Rose*.

FAMOUS SHIPS

Mary Rose

Launched in 1511, the four-master *Mary Rose* was one of the first sailing warships capable of firing a broadside (the simultaneous firing of all guns from one side of a warship), owing to the newly developed gun ports on the ships of the time. Over the next thirty-three years she gained fame and glory in several wars against France, Scotland and Brittany, so it would have been no surprise to see her leading the attack alongside *Henri Grace à Dieu* against the French at the Battle of the Solent in 1545.

Early in the battle, though, something went disastrously wrong as she suddenly heeled over to her starboard side and sank. Only thirty-five men out of a crew of more than 400 survived, many of them being crushed or trapped by the heavy guns and other equipment that slid down from the port side, with many others drowning below decks or unable to make their way through the heavy anti-boarding netting that covered the upper decks. The cause of her sinking was water flooding into her open gun ports on the starboard side and there remain many theories about why that should have happened, including an incompetent crew, the ship being overloaded, turning too hard to avoid the nearby Spitbank or a direct hit by French cannon shot.

Salvage attempts in the aftermath of the battle failed because the ship had quickly embedded itself deep into the clay of the seabed, and it was 1982 before modern methods and much determination and funding resulted in the *Mary Rose* returning to the surface. Following her subsequent painstaking preservation, she is now on display at the Portsmouth Historic Dockyard.

1546:   The Anthony Roll, a beautifully illustrated inventory of the fifty-eight ships of the Tudor Navy at the time, was presented to Henry VIII. It was named after its creator, Anthony Anthony, who produced his magnum opus on three rolls of vellum which survive to this day. In 1680 the first and third rolls were given by Charles II to Samuel Pepys, who had them cut up and reproduced as a single-volume book, which now resides in the Pepys Library at Magdalene College in Cambridge. The second roll was sold to the British Museum by a daughter of William IV in 1858 and is now owned by the British Library.

1578:   John Hawkins, already an experienced mariner as a privateer and slave trader licensed by Elizabeth I, was appointed Treasurer of the Navy, a position he used to make a great many improvements to the Elizabethan Navy over the next decade.

⚓ FAMOUS SAILORS ⚓

SIR JOHN HAWKINS
(1532–95)

The remarkable improvements John Hawkins made to the Elizabethan Navy included the following.

► Technical improvements to the ships, including a streamlining of their profile and the introduction of full rigging, which meant the sails could be reconfigured quickly according to weather and battle conditions. The fleet became faster and more manoeuvrable than anything else at sea.

► The development and introduction of lighter cannons that could be reloaded and fired at much shorter intervals than ever before.

► A pay increase for sailors – he was one of the first men in the country to recognise the link between pay, motivation and performance.

► A charity for the relief of sick, injured, disabled or elderly mariners, which continues to this day as the Hospital of Sir John Hawkins, Knight, in Chatham.

In addition to being the chief architect of a revamped Elizabethan Navy, Hawkins personally engaged in international espionage against the Spanish and served as the Member of Parliament for Plymouth. He was also an excellent naval commander, which would later result in his appointment as third-in-command against the Spanish Armada in 1588, the same year in which he was knighted.

1580: After three years on board the *Golden Hind*, Francis Drake became the first Englishman to have captained a circumnavigation of the globe. He also found time to plunder some Spanish treasure off the west coast of the Americas while he was about it.

⚓ FAMOUS SAILORS ⚓

SIR FRANCIS DRAKE
(1540–96)

Francis Drake was a sea captain in the Elizabethan Navy, knighted by Elizabeth I for his circumnavigation of the globe and for swelling her coffers with the plunder he gained as a licensed privateer and slave trader. His naval accomplishments included several pre-emptive strikes that delayed the Spanish Armada setting sail for a year,

> and which became known as 'the singeing of the King of Spain's beard'. There is some doubt as to whether he finished a game of bowls in Plymouth Hoe before joining his ship to engage with the approaching Spanish Armada the following year, but there is no doubt that he played a major part in the engagement, not least when he put the Spanish into disarray by sending fireships amongst them on the eve of battle.

1588:   The 130 ships of the Spanish Armada set off with the primary objective of picking up soldiers stationed in the Spanish Netherlands and transporting them across the English Channel to invade England. Only then could they overthrow the English queen, put a stop to what they saw as the vile disease of Protestantism and prevent the likes of Francis Drake and John Hawkins from plundering their ships and colonies around the world.

GREAT SEA BATTLES
THE BATTLE OF GRAVELINES (1588)

On the morning of 8 August 1588, the Spanish Armada found itself at a disadvantage off Gravelines on the coast of the Spanish Netherlands, in spite of having fifty per cent greater firepower than the English fleet. Some bad weather on the way across the Bay of Biscay – along with a certain amount of indecision, poor communication and inferior tactics once they had reached the English Channel – had left their ships vulnerable, on top of which they had been scattered by Drake's fireship attack the night before.

Thanks to the technical improvements that had been brought about by John Hawkins over the previous ten years, the English ships were also faster and more manoeuvrable, allowing their superior cannons to fire broadsides from an upwind position while maintaining sufficient distance to avoid the prospect of being boarded. Within eight hours, five of the Spanish ships had been lost and the rest were in disarray, all hope of invading England now gone. Their only hope of escape was to travel northwards around Scotland and then to the west of Ireland, but ferocious Atlantic storms battered them on to rocks or forced them aground, resulting in around 5,000 men being drowned, lost to starvation or slaughtered.

THE ENGLISH CIVIL WAR AND THE COMMONWEALTH (1642-60)

When the English Civil War broke out in 1642, the Navy sided with the Parliamentarians, although some of the fleet later mutinied to join the Royalists. The Parliamentarians made themselves rather unpopular abroad after executing Charles I in 1649 (it probably made a lot of other kings and queens nervous), and the Navy had to be expanded to cope with England's growing number of actual and potential enemies. The Commonwealth regime of Oliver Cromwell in the 1650s created the most powerful and effective navy the country had yet seen, and the man largely responsible was Robert Blake.

⚓ FAMOUS SAILORS ⚓

ROBERT BLAKE
(1599–1657)

Robert Blake was the most distinguished General-at-Sea (Parliamentarian speak for 'Admiral') throughout the Commonwealth period. He improved naval tactics in his Fighting Instructions and introduced the 'line of battle' formation, a tactic which prevented the unwanted consequences of 'friendly fire'. He imposed the first-ever set of naval rules and regulations, including trial and sentence by court martial, to improve discipline and efficiency.

He also established British supremacy at sea, with notable victories over Portugal, Spain and the Netherlands during his tenure between 1649 and 1657. His most famous action was at the Battle of Santa Cruz off the Canary Islands in 1657, where sixteen Spanish ships were destroyed, the heaviest defeat of the Spanish since the Armada of 1588, and one which left that country's finances in ruin.

For a while his remarkable achievements were largely forgotten by history, in line with the general policy to discredit all Parliamentarians following the restoration of the monarchy, but he has since been recognised, with several ships named after him, a stone memorial in Westminster Abbey, a statue in Bridgwater, Somerset (his place of birth), a 1982 postage stamp and an oilfield in the North Sea. Perhaps the best accolade of all, though, was the admission by Lord Nelson that he did not consider himself the equal of Blake after losing his left arm in a failed attack on Santa Cruz, the scene of Blake's greatest triumph.

THE RISE OF THE ROYAL NAVY AND THE NAPOLEONIC WARS (1660–1815)

*Tell the surgeon to make haste and get his
instruments. I know I must lose my right
arm, so the sooner it is off the better.*

HORATIO NELSON

Once General George Monck had decided in 1660 that an unstable parliament was even worse than an unstable monarchy, he arranged for Charles II to return from exile so that the monarchy could be restored. Parliament agreed, subject to certain conditions that included the need for the Navy to be a national institution renewable each year only through an Act of Parliament, as opposed to remaining a crown possession (although, ironically, nobody seemed to mind it having the word 'royal' in its new title). The 'Royal Navy' was born and, after some initial reversals, it would go from strength to strength during the Georgian era, until it emerged triumphant and all-powerful from the Napoleonic Wars just over 150 years later.

THE PROFESSIONALS

The battle for worldwide naval supremacy was fought by Britain, France, Portugal and the Netherlands through many wars in Europe and beyond in the seventeenth and eighteenth centuries. Naval design, firepower and tactics remained as important as ever, but gaining the ascendancy now depended on a more sophisticated game plan, requiring increasingly cohesive organisation, allegiances, financing, logistics, medical care, hygiene, training and dockyard facilities. In other words, it was time to get professional.

1660:   Samuel Pepys was appointed to the Navy Board in the same year he started writing his famous diaries. His writings are best known for their coverage of the Great Plague (1665–66) and the Great Fire of London (1666), but he also wrote extensively about the Second Anglo-Dutch War (1665–67) from a naval perspective, something that would stand him in good stead when he was appointed Chief Secretary to the Admiralty in 1673.

1664:   The Marines were formed in 1664 as the Duke of York and Albany's Maritime Regiment of Foot (their name being changed to the Royal Marines by George III in 1802).

1667:   The Raid on the Medway off Chatham Dockyard was one of the worst naval reversals in British history.

The Dutch attacked and destroyed eleven ships, including some of the Navy's largest warships, while they were mothballed awaiting funding. The humiliation became overwhelming when the Dutch captured and towed away as prizes HMS *Unity* and the flagship of the English fleet, HMS *Royal Charles*, but lessons would be learned from this setback.

⚓ SAMUEL PEPYS ⚓
(1633–1703)

Samuel Pepys rose to be Chief Secretary to the Admiralty under Charles II and James II despite having no maritime experience. What he did have was a natural-born talent for administration, and the reforms he brought about were instrumental in the professionalisation of the Navy. Learning from mistakes made during the Second Anglo-Dutch War and being acutely aware that the Dutch Navy had recently become superior to the newly formed Royal Navy in many respects, he introduced or contributed to the following important reforms.

► A centralised approach to supplying the fleet, thereby increasing efficiency and reducing theft and corruption.

► An improved standard of food supplied to ships' crews.

► The establishment of the Royal Mathematical School to train forty boys each year in navigation, and the replacement of its master with someone who knew a bit more about the sea.

► The creation of exams, including for navigation and mathematics.

► More practical experience of the sea for naval commanders.

► The setting of minimum standards for ships' surgeons, pursers and even parsons.

1688–97: Following the Glorious Revolution of 1688, in which the Catholic James II was overthrown by a combination of English Parliamentarians and the Protestant William III of Orange (who was already married to Mary, the daughter of James II), an Anglo-Dutch alliance was formed to contest the ensuing Nine Years' War against France. After a worrying French victory at the Battle of Beachy Head (1690), the combined Anglo-Dutch fleet rallied to win convincingly at the Battles of Barfleur and La Hogue in 1692, ending France's brief period of naval dominance and averting the latest planned invasion of England.

1704: The Anglo-Dutch fleet captured Gibraltar from Spain during the War of the Spanish Succession. It was during this action and the long siege that followed that the Marines first made a name for themselves as an elite fighting force. The territory was ceded to Britain in perpetuity at the end of the war in 1714 and the Navy still maintains a squadron there today.

1707:   The Acts of Union created the Kingdom of Great Britain, and the Royal Navy and Royal Scots Navy were accordingly merged.

NAVY SPEAK
JACK

The 'Jack' nickname for male sailors in the Navy derived from 'Jack Tar', the term used for eighteenth-century matelots (sailors), who wore a glossy black hat and coiffured pigtails. Their hair and clothes were waterproofed with the tar that gave them the original nickname.

The related term 'Jack of all trades' came from the fact that a sailor had to be able to turn his hand to many different jobs. Unlike in the Army, which had separate infantry, cavalry and artillery regiments, the Jacks of the Navy had to provide all features of military operations by themselves.

All large organisations end up with their peculiar slang to communicate with one another and the Navy is no exception. Perhaps it is unsurprising that 'Jackspeak' is the name they gave to it.

THE WAR OF JENKINS' EAR (1739–48)

This war is remembered mostly for the manner in which it came about. At a time when the British and the Spanish really weren't getting on very well with one another, a Spanish commander boarded the British merchant brig *Rebecca* off the coast of Florida and sliced off the ear of her captain, Robert Jenkins, on the grounds that he was smuggling. When Jenkins ultimately reported this to Parliament, it was taken as the latest in a long line of Spanish insults, and war was accordingly declared on Spain.

The war itself was also fought in the Americas, with neither side gaining much advantage, although one British success at Portobelo in Panama was so popular back home that the poem 'Rule Britannia' was set to music and sung in public for the first time at a dinner to honour Edward Vernon, the vice admiral responsible for the victory. London's Portobello Road and the Edinburgh suburb of Portobello were both named after the battle.

⚓ FAMOUS SAILORS ⚓

ADMIRAL GEORGE ANSON
(1697–1762)

George Anson saw action as a junior officer during the War of the Spanish Succession and the defeat of the Spanish at the Battle of Cape Passaro during the War of the Quadruple Alliance (a war in which Britain, France, Austria and the Dutch Republic ganged up on Spain to stop it invading Italy in addition to claiming the French throne).

Having been promoted to Commodore, he set off in 1740, during the War of Jenkins' Ear, on a circumnavigation of the globe. Against all the odds, his fleet having been decimated by storms and many of his crew having mutinied or died of scurvy, he captured a Spanish galleon off the Philippines laden with 1,313,843 pieces of eight (the Spanish dollar) and carrying sea charts that greatly added to British knowledge of the Pacific Islands. He returned in 1744 with just one of the eight ships and about ten per cent of the 2,000 or so men he had originally left with, but he was now a rich man and he was promoted to vice admiral for his efforts.

He commanded the fleet that defeated the French at the First Battle of Finisterre (1747) off the coast of northwest Spain during the War of the Austrian Succession, capturing four ships of the line, two frigates and seven merchant vessels. The main point of the battle had been to curtail trade between France and its empire overseas, and Anson was raised to the peerage as a result of what was an important victory in that respect.

Appointed First Lord of the Admiralty in 1751, he masterminded operations throughout the Seven Years' War and also instigated a number of far-reaching reforms.

- ▶ A revision of the Articles of War to tighten discipline throughout the Navy.

- ▶ Improved medical care.

- ▶ Uniforms for commissioned officers.

- ▶ The removal of corrupt defence contractors.

- ▶ The system of rating ships according to the number of guns they carried.

- ▶ The transfer of the Marines from the Army into the Navy.

- ▶ The establishment of a permanent squadron at Devonport in order to better control the western approaches to Britain.

THE SEVEN YEARS' WAR (1756-63)

At the start of the Seven Years' War, the French Navy had still not fully recovered from the War of the Austrian Succession (Rear-Admiral Edward Hawke had taken up where George Anson had left off by inflicting another heavy defeat on the French at the Second Battle of Finisterre in 1747). The war, however, got off to a bad start for Britain when Admiral Byng failed to put an end to the French Siege of Minorca. Following his court martial and execution by firing squad for not having tried hard enough, largely due to Anson's revised Articles of War, it became a standing joke in France that the British sometimes killed their own admirals *pour encourager les autres* (to encourage the others).

The rest of the war went better, with the French soundly defeated at the Battle of Quiberon Bay and the Spanish relieved of Havana and Manila (which Britain later swapped for Florida), primarily due to better support for the fleet as the war wore on. It may also have helped that the remaining admirals knew only too well that feedback from the Admiralty on their performance might not always have been as constructive as they would have liked, with little opportunity offered to learn from past mistakes.

GREAT SEA BATTLES
THE BATTLE OF QUIBERON BAY (1759)

The Battle of Quiberon Bay off the coast of Brittany was one of the most decisive victories in British naval history, with the twenty-three ships of the line of Admiral Edward Hawke outsailing and outfighting the French fleet in violent weather. The twenty-one French ships were either destroyed, blockaded or only able to make their escape over the shallows after jettisoning their cannons. Not only was Britain once more saved from possible invasion but the French were once more left in a weakened state, barely able to fight on in Europe and unable to send adequate supplies and reinforcements to their overseas territories, which would soon lose them a number of their colonies, including Canada.

⚓ FAMOUS SAILORS ⚓

ADMIRAL RICHARD HOWE
(1726–99)

Richard Howe gained recognition during the Seven Years' War by capturing a French gunship off Newfoundland with the first shot fired in the war. He also excelled during amphibious operations against the French coast (something of a transformation for the Navy at the time) and led the fleet of Admiral Hawke in the decisive victory at Quiberon Bay.

The part he played in the blockade of the American coastline during the American Revolutionary War resulted in the capture of Long Island and New York City, and he went on to relieve the long-running Siege of Gibraltar in that same war, despite being greatly outnumbered by French and Spanish ships of the line.

Howe's finest hour came in 1794 when he commanded the victorious fleet at the Glorious First of June battle (see below), following which he was promoted to Admiral of the Fleet. His swansong was the pacification of the Spithead mutineers in 1797 after twelve hours of listening to the grievances of the men concerned while being rowed around the fleet.

⚓ FAMOUS SAILORS ⚓

CAPTAIN JAMES COOK
(1728–79)

James Cook saw action as a ship's master (a naval officer responsible for the navigation of a ship) in Canada during the Seven Years' War, including the amphibious assault on the Fortress of Louisburg, the Siege of Quebec and the Battle of the Plains of Abraham. It was he who surveyed and led the fleet up the St Lawrence River to Quebec, delivering General James Wolfe and his army to the position from which they wrested control of Canada from the French.

Cook went on to become one of Britain's greatest ever explorers, an excellent navigator, surveyor and cartographer who greatly improved the Navy's understanding of the southern hemisphere. In completing three circumnavigations of the globe, he claimed New South Wales in Australia for Britain and was the first explorer to cross the Antarctic Circle, circumnavigate New Zealand and map out the Hawaiian islands.

He met with an unfortunate end when he was killed during a riot by Hawaiian natives following an argument over a stolen boat.

JOHN HARRISON (1693-1776) AND THE H4 CHRONOMETER

John Harrison was an English clockmaker who, in the 1760s, invented the first practical marine chronometer, the H4, to solve the problem of identifying longitude at sea. Ocean-going ships lucky enough to have one on board (the early versions cost a third as much as the ships they were used on) were less likely to miss their destination or flounder on uncharted rocks. It was the most important advance in marine navigation since early sailors had figured out how to navigate approximately by means of celestial observation alone, and it would remain the mainstay of marine navigation throughout the age of sail. James Cook used a copy of the H4 to calculate his longitude during his second circumnavigation, and in due course affordable versions of the timepiece would be used across the Navy.

NAVY SPEAK
LIMEYS

While serving as a ship's surgeon in 1747, James Lind (1716–94) carried out experiments into the cause of scurvy, the symptoms of which include loose teeth, bleeding gums and haemorrhages. He correctly identified citrus fruits as an effective remedy for the disease (nowadays we know that scurvy is caused by a lack of vitamin C, but vitamins would not be identified until the twentieth century).

Building on Lind's findings, James Cook travelled 70,000 miles between 1771 and 1774 with no deaths from scurvy on account of the many different foods with which he tried to prevent or cure the disease. He reported his findings to the Royal Society, and scurvy was finally eradicated from the Navy twenty years later after physician Gilbert Blane, a commissioner on the Navy's Sick and Hurt Board, ordered lemon juice to be given to all sailors at sea. Lemons were later replaced by limes, which were more readily available in the Caribbean colonies, resulting in the slang word 'limey' to describe British sailors and later all British people.

TAKING CONTROL OF THE SEAS

By concentrating its military resources on the Navy in the eighteenth century – which it could do because it didn't have any land borders to defend – Britain had become rich by controlling the important trade routes. It was also able to drop off its relatively small but highly mobile army anywhere in the world – and keep it furnished with supplies and reinforcements where and when needed. Notwithstanding the odd mutiny over pay and conditions, the Navy could also man its fleet relatively easily compared to other nations, through a mixture of conscription (each county had to supply a quota according to its population and number of ports), press-ganging and volunteers from around Britain and further afield. American, Dutch, Scandinavian and Italian sailors all volunteered for the Royal Navy, and even French sailors were persuaded to jump aboard after their own ships had been sunk or captured. To consolidate this naval supremacy, though, there were the small matters of the French Revolutionary and Napoleonic Wars to contend with.

NAVY SPEAK
THE 'ANDREW'

The 'Andrew' is a common nickname for the Navy and is thought to derive from either Andrew Walker, who press-ganged so many men in the eighteenth century that the Navy was said to be 'Andrew's' as opposed to 'His Majesty's', or Andrew Miller, who had a monopoly to supply provisions to the Navy's warships at the time of the Napoleonic Wars.

FRENCH REVOLUTIONARY AND NAPOLEONIC WARS (1793–1815)

The Navy enjoyed a series of remarkable successes during the French Revolutionary and Napoleonic Wars, reaching a real high with Lord Nelson's victory at the Battle of Trafalgar, which pretty much ended any further contest at sea for the next hundred years.

GREAT SEA BATTLES

THE BATTLES OF THE FRENCH REVOLUTIONARY AND NAPOLEONIC WARS (1793–1815)

THE BATTLE OF THE GLORIOUS FIRST OF JUNE (1794)

The first naval engagement of the French Revolutionary Wars saw Admiral Richard Howe's Channel Fleet soundly defeat the French Atlantic Fleet of Admiral Villaret de Joyeuse 400 miles to the west of Brittany. Although the French grain convoy did get through that day, which prevented mass starvation across France, it was the worst tactical loss the French Navy had suffered in a single day in over a hundred years, with one ship sunk, six ships and 3,000 men captured, and 4,000 casualties. British casualties were 1,200, with no ships lost (although many were damaged). The fleets had been evenly matched, but Howe won the day with the surprise tactic of raking the French ships across the narrower bow or stern on a one-to-one basis instead of lining up for the usual line-of-battle broadside firing of cannons.

THE BATTLE OF CAPE ST VINCENT (1797)

Because the Spanish had thrown their lot in with the French, the British Mediterranean Fleet under Admiral Sir John Jervis, on board his flagship HMS *Victory*, sought to engage the Spanish fleet off Cape St Vincent on the south-western tip of Portugal. It was only when heavy fog lifted that Jervis realised he was outnumbered by thirty-six ships to twenty-two, but he secured a famous victory against the odds thanks to superior tactics and a more experienced command and crew. He was also helped by the initiative and daring of Captain Horatio Nelson, who had already lost his sight in one eye after being injured by an exploding sandbag while besieging Corsica in 1794, but who broke from the line in HMS *Captain* to engage much larger ships when he saw that they were trying to escape. His heroic action resulted in two of the larger Spanish ships being captured, and it made his name and earned him his knighthood. The boarding of the much larger *San Nicolas* was so impressive that it passed into folklore as 'Nelson's Patent Bridge for Boarding First Rates' ('First Rate' was the designation for the largest ships of the line, meaning they had over a hundred guns and around 800 officers and men).

THE BATTLE OF THE NILE (1798)
Also known as the Battle of Aboukir Bay, this battle against the French took place in the Mediterranean, just off the Nile Delta. Rear Admiral Horatio Nelson, now minus the right arm that he had lost the year before at the Battle of Santa Cruz de Tenerife, had just spent two months pursuing the French fleet that had carried Napoleon Bonaparte and his expeditionary force to Egypt.

When he finally caught up with the French, Nelson attacked immediately, even though it was approaching dusk. He caught the enemy in crossfire by splitting his own fleet into two and battered them into surrender. The French flagship *Orient* exploded, and only four out of seventeen French ships escaped the battle. It was the turning point of the French Revolutionary Wars in Britain's favour, leading Nelson to quote from Shakespeare's *Henry V* as he described the captains who served with him that day as his 'Band of Brothers'.

Nelson was once more injured after a piece of French shot struck him in the forehead, but relatively minor surgery soon had him sewn back up. By now he was an acclaimed hero across Europe, showered with presents from the likes of the Tsar of Russia and the Sultan of the Ottoman Empire.

THE BATTLE OF COPENHAGEN (1801)
A British fleet under Admiral Sir Hyde Parker was despatched to engage a Danish fleet off Copenhagen after Denmark had joined with Russia,

Prussia and Sweden to resist a British embargo of free trade with France. Vice Admiral Horatio Nelson led the attack and famously fought on in this, his toughest battle to date, after ignoring an order to disengage (legend has it that he did so by raising his telescope to his blind eye to avoid reading the signal from Parker). Nelson finally managed to force a truce and a strategic victory after many hours of fierce fighting. Fifteen of the Danish ships were sunk, exploded or captured, but most of the British ships were also seriously damaged.

THE BATTLE OF TRAFALGAR (1805)

The Battle of Trafalgar was fought in the Atlantic, just off Cape Trafalgar on the south-west coast of Spain. Admiral Lord Nelson was up against a numerically superior Franco-Spanish fleet, but he was used to that by now, and it didn't prevent him from inflicting one more crushing defeat on the enemy before finally succumbing to a musket-ball wound on board his flagship HMS *Victory*.

The Franco-Spanish fleet lost around half their ships, while the British fleet lost none, a definitive victory achieved once more through Nelson's innovative tactics of getting in amongst the enemy by attacking swiftly in two columns – he had previously arranged for the British ships to be painted in a distinctive yellow and black pattern to avoid shooting at one another in the confusion of such a close battle. The British cause was also helped by the fact that many of the most experienced French naval commanders had been executed during the French Revolution, something which Nelson intended to take full advantage of. It was the most decisive naval battle of the Napoleonic Wars and ended Napoleon's chances of invading Britain once and for all.

Ships captured at the time were sold and the proceeds distributed to everyone who had fought on the winning side, but many of the ships that were taken at Trafalgar were destroyed in a storm not long after the battle. To compensate for this misfortune, Parliament made a special grant of £300,000 and even the most junior ranks ended up receiving several months' pay.

A FOOTNOTE TO THE BATTLE OF TRAFALGAR

On 13 September 1805 Lord Nelson visited James Lock and Co. Hatters in London for the last time to order a new 7 1/8 full cocked hat of the finest beaver fur, with a cockade and loop of navy-blue silk. In other words, it was the usual order for his signature bicorne, but with an in-built eye-shade (after losing the sight of one eye during the Siege of Corsica, he wanted to guard against the same thing happening to the other one). Because Nelson was about to set off for Spain to engage the Franco-Spanish fleet, he paid the bill in full there and then, but he never did get to wear his new hat because the following month he lost his life at the Battle of Trafalgar, wearing the hat that James Lock and Co. had made for him two years previously.

NAVY SPEAK
TURN A BLIND EYE

When Nelson deliberately ignored the order to break away from battle at Copenhagen, he inspired the phrase that still exists today to explain the need to sometimes ignore a misdemeanour or instruction in favour of getting the right longer-term result.

⚓ FAMOUS SAILORS ⚓

ADMIRAL LORD NELSON
(1758–1805)

Horatio Nelson was born in Norfolk, the sixth child of a church minister, and joined the Navy at the tender age of twelve as a midshipman (the lowest officer rank in the Navy).

Ultimately renowned for his unfailing courage, inspirational leadership, strategic awareness and tactical prowess, he became the greatest officer the Navy ever had. It is difficult to imagine a more determined human being than Nelson: he didn't just work his way up the ranks to secure four remarkable victories in the French Revolutionary and Napoleonic Wars – he did so against the odds and against everything the gods could throw at him.

You might reasonably have expected him to seek out medical retirement after some awful injuries: losing his sight in one eye; having his right forearm amputated at a time when that probably hurt a lot; and carrying on as if nothing had happened while the skin of his forehead flapped about below a gaping head wound. Unbelievably, though, his toughest victories were still to come at Copenhagen and Trafalgar.

It is well documented that Nelson had to overcome, on a regular basis, seasickness, toothache, dysentery, malaria, gout, palpitations and breathlessness. By the time he met Emma Hamilton, the love of his life, he had lost many of his teeth and was showing signs of premature ageing, but he wooed her regardless, and she was soon smitten by the sheer presence of the man.

Given his many injuries and illnesses, you could almost be forgiven for thinking that Nelson was not a man who was cut out for a life at sea, but they probably couldn't find a medical officer brave enough to tell him that.

Nelson was accorded a state funeral and buried in St Paul's Cathedral, having been brought home preserved in a barrel of brandy, and numerous monuments were created in his memory, including Nelson's Column in Trafalgar Square and the Nelson Monument in Edinburgh (many Scots fought at Trafalgar). The four panels around the plinth of Nelson's Column in London were made from the melted-down bronze of captured French cannons and depict his four greatest victories: at Cape St Vincent, the Nile, Copenhagen and Trafalgar.

FAMOUS SHIPS

HMS *Victory*

Ordered by Prime Minister William Pitt the Elder in 1758 and launched at Chatham Dockyard in 1765, HMS *Victory* was built from 2,000 oak trees, 27 miles of rope rigging and 4 acres of canvas sails. She was a 104-gun first-rate ship of the line, which is another way of saying she was big and purpose built to wage war.

She is best remembered as Nelson's flagship at Trafalgar in 1805, but she had in fact seen serious action as Britain's flagship in four battles before that. Her battle CV reads as follows:

Battle	Commander	War
First Battle of Ushant (1778)	Augustus Keppel	Anglo-French War
Second Battle of Ushant (1781)	Richard Kempenfelt	Anglo-French War
Battle of Cape Spartel (1782)	Richard Howe	American Revolutionary War
Battle of Cape St Vincent (1797)	Sir John Jervis	French Revolutionary Wars
Battle of Trafalgar (1805)	Thomas Hardy	Napoleonic Wars

Having served as a harbour ship following the end of her active life in 1812, *Victory* was finally moved to dry-dock in Portsmouth Harbour in 1922, where she remains as a museum ship and, since 2012, as the flagship of the First Sea Lord. Having survived a hit by the Luftwaffe in 1941, and thanks to a major ongoing programme of preservation, she remains the world's oldest naval ship still in commission.

⚓ FAMOUS SAILORS ⚓

ADMIRAL THOMAS COCHRANE
(1775–1860)

Thomas Cochrane fought with such distinction during the Napoleonic Wars that Napoleon referred to him as *Le Loup des Mers* (Sea Wolf), but his remarkable career was brought to a shuddering halt in 1814 when he was wrongly jailed for fraud on the Stock Exchange and stripped of his naval rank.

Not a man to sit around sulking, he spent several years organising and leading the Chilean and Brazilian Navies to successfully gain independence from their Spanish and Portuguese masters respectively. He also used the Brazilian Navy to help liberate Peru from the Spanish and later organised and advised the Greek Navy during their War of Independence, which was fought to escape the clutches of the Ottoman Empire.

His British Navy rank was restored after he received a long overdue royal pardon in 1832, and to this day the Chilean Navy still lay wreaths each year at his grave in Westminster Abbey. Cochrane has been immortalised in numerous books and poems, and the character and career of C. S. Forester's fictional hero Horatio Hornblower are in part modelled on him. He is also one of the main characters portrayed in Bernard Cornwell's novel *Sharpe's Devil*.

THE AMERICAN WAR (1812–15)

Increasing tension at sea between Britain and the USA led to the American War, which played out on the Great Lakes, in the Caribbean and off the east coast of America. Much blockading of trade routes was the order of the day, but there were also some significant battles – the most morale-boosting of which, from a British point of view, was the straight fight between HMS *Shannon* and the USS *Chesapeake*.

GREAT SEA BATTLES
THE CAPTURE OF USS *CHESAPEAKE* (1813)

The sailing frigates HMS *Shannon* and USS *Chesapeake* were evenly matched in terms of size and gun power when they lined up against one another for what would be a brief but bloody ship-to-ship battle to the east of Boston. Although there was a larger crew on the *Chesapeake*, the commander of the *Shannon*, Captain Philip Broke, had his men better trained – and that made the difference. They fired their cannons with greater accuracy and were also lightning fast at boarding for close combat. Such was the ferocity of the fighting that eighty men were killed and 154 wounded in the fifteen minutes that it took the British to disable, board and capture the *Chesapeake* from the time the first cannon shots were fired. The captain of the *Chesapeake*, James Lawrence, was killed. Broke himself was seriously injured, but surgeons worked on him on the way to Halifax, Nova Scotia, where he recovered.

MAINTAINING NAVAL SUPREMACY INTO THE AGE OF STEEL AND STEAM (1815–1914)

The essence of war is violence.
Moderation in war is imbecility.

'JACKY' FISHER

For a hundred years after the end of the Napoleonic Wars, Britannia did indeed rule the waves, although it was hardly plain sailing as the technology morphed into steel and steam. It was the period known as Pax Britannica due to the 'world policeman' role that Britain took upon itself to perform. The political world was volatile, which meant that the Navy couldn't be sure from one year to the next which countries would be friends and which would be foes, resulting in some unexpected coalitions against some unexpected enemies. They got involved pretty much everywhere in the world, according to which ruler was the latest to become a bit too big for his boots.

THE BLOCKADE OF AFRICA (1808-60)

As one of the first nations to end its own involvement in the slave trade when it passed the Abolition of the Slave Trade Act in 1807, Britain led the drive to put an end to the transatlantic nightmare. It was to become the longest campaign in the Navy's history. Over the next four decades, they captured 160 slave ships and freed 150,000 Africans, although they did pay a heavy price for their success, losing more than 17,000 men in the process, many to disease.

In one significant action in 1816, an Anglo-Dutch fleet under Admiral Lord Exmouth bombarded the harbour and ships of Algiers to encourage the Dey of Algiers to put an end to his country's ongoing practices of slavery and piracy on the high seas.

GREAT SEA BATTLES
THE BATTLE OF NAVARINO (1827)

Fought during the Greek War of Independence, the Battle of Navarino took place just off the Peloponnese peninsula. It was the final major sea battle of the age of sail, even if most ships did fight at anchor within the bay. A coalition of British, Russian and French ships led by Vice Admiral Sir Edward Codrington soundly defeated those of the Ottoman-Egyptian fleet, which had been despatched to put down the Greek push for independence from the Ottoman Empire.

The Allies under Codrington had only twenty-two ships and 1,258 guns against the seventy-eight ships and 2,180 guns of the enemy, but bigger ships, greater firepower and better-trained gunners afforded them the upper hand. A massacre ensued, and within two hours only eight Ottoman-Egyptian ships remained seaworthy.

THE FIRST OPIUM WAR (1839-42)

After the Chinese government tried to restrain Britain's trade into China, and in particular its lucrative opium trade from India, the Navy was despatched to blockade Canton and bombard a number of coastal towns, as a result of which Britain gained its base in Hong Kong.

THE BOMBARDMENT OF ACRE (1840)

The Bombardment of Acre took place to put Muhammad Ali, the Viceroy of Egypt, back in his place after he had captured Acre (in what was then Syria) and declared his own country's independence from the Ottoman Empire. The British fleet, commanded by Admiral Sir Robert Stopford and supported by small Austrian and Ottoman squadrons, took just 2 hours 20 minutes to silence the Egyptian coastal defences. The efficiency of the operation was down to the Navy's ability to fire off a whopping 48,000 rounds in that time, not least because of the training their gunners had received at the Naval School of Gunnery, which had been running since 1829 on board the converted HMS *Excellent* at Whale Island in Portsmouth.

NAVAL BRIGADES

Between 1850 and 1914 the Navy fought only one ship-to-ship battle at sea, in 1877 against a Peruvian ironclad (a steam-propelled warship protected by iron or steel plates of armour). Not wanting to have its officers and crew idle, it was a regular occurrence for the Navy to form temporary detachments of Royal Marines and Royal Navy seamen to fight on land. These detachments were known as Naval Brigades and saw action in fifteen different wars during that period, including the Crimean War, the Second Opium War, the Indian Mutiny, the Zulu War, the Second Boer War and the Boxer Rebellion.

CRIMEAN WAR (1853-56)

The Crimean War was fought to curb Russian expansion and prevent it from gaining access to a warm-water port from which it could move freely into the Mediterranean. In addition to transporting land forces around the Black Sea, the Royal Navy and French Navy bombarded Odessa and laid siege to Sevastopol in 1853, which resulted in the Russians scuttling their entire fleet there. During the

Sea of Azov Campaign in 1855, British and French warships struck at almost every Russian town, depot, building or fortification along the coastline, cutting off supplies to Russian land forces and thereby making a significant contribution to overall victory by 1856.

FAMOUS SHIPS

HMS *Warrior* (1860)

When she was launched in 1860 at Bow Creek in London, HMS *Warrior* was the first wrought-iron-hulled, armour-plated, steam-powered warship the world had seen, but she still looked a bit like an old-fashioned sailing ship – because she was that too, having a broadside gun arrangement and three masts to carry her sails. The sails were useful as backup and because a combination of steam and sail could increase overall speed from 14 knots to as much as 20 knots.

She never saw direct action, but she did serve as a necessary deterrent, and she carried out some useful tasks, like towing a floating dry dock to Bermuda and escorting the Princess Alexandra from Denmark to Britain to marry the Prince of Wales (the future King Edward VII).

Although *Warrior* led the way in modern battleship design, and was therefore an essential stepping stone along the way, the pace of technology was such that she started to become obsolete within ten years of her launch, and she also suffered some moments of ignominy during her brief life.

▶ She was launched during the coldest winter for fifty years and had become frozen to her slipway. Hydraulic rams and extra tugs were used to gain forward momentum, but she still had to be rocked free by dock workers running from side to side on the upper deck – probably not a comedy moment the Navy had hoped for while launching the world's most advanced battleship.

▶ The length and weight of the ship meant she was difficult to manoeuvre, resulting in an accidental ramming of HMS *Royal Oak* while they were en route to Scotland in 1868, when *Warrior* lost her figurehead and jib boom.

▶ She narrowly missed colliding with HMS *Agincourt* in 1870 while they were leaving Gibraltar together, forcing *Agincourt* to take evasive action and run herself aground.

After performing various harbour duties for much of the twentieth century, she is now a magnificent museum ship at Portsmouth Historic Dockyard, complete with a replacement figurehead that was the subject of much media attention when it was carved in the 1980s.

NAVY SPEAK
A FAIR RATE OF KNOTS

The term 'knot', shorthand for 'nautical mile per hour' (the equivalent of 1.15 miles per hour on land), derives from the days of sail. Navigators measured their speed through the water by a series of knots in a reel of string fed out over the stern of the ship over a set period measured by a sandglass. 'Moving at a fair rate of knots' later found its way into common English as an alternative way to say 'moving very quickly'.

HMS *DEVASTATION*

Launched in 1871, HMS *Devastation* was the first leading battleship of the Navy not to carry sails, changing the profile of warships for ever. The absence of masts allowed guns to be mounted in revolving turrets on top of the hull for the first time. Many of the naval officers of the time hated this image of modernity, considering it a monstrosity and hankering after the days of sail and miles of rigging.

The iconic image and name of the ship has been portrayed on England's Glory matchboxes for a century and a half, although they are now produced in Sweden, which arguably lessens the glory somewhat.

TAKING ON BOARD THE BRILLIANT IDEA OF JOSEPH SWAN (1828–1914)

Within a year of Joseph Swan inventing the incandescent light bulb in 1880 (his house in Gateshead was the first in the world to be lit in this way), the Navy started to instal them on their ships, beginning with the ironclad battleship HMS *Inflexible*. Electric lighting unfortunately led to the first fatal electrocution on board a Navy ship in 1882, following which the standard voltage was reduced from 800 to 80.

THE BOMBARDMENT OF ALEXANDRIA (1882)

The Bombardment of Alexandria was undertaken to quell an Egyptian nationalist uprising, which had resulted in anti-Christian riots and the fortification of the harbour at Alexandria, and which threatened Britain's reliance on the Suez Canal for trade and military purposes. Admiral Beauchamp Seymour commanded the British Mediterranean Fleet of fifteen ironclad ships, whose superior firepower over the harbour defences left the ultimate result of the engagement in little doubt.

THE BUILD-UP TO WORLD WAR ONE

The Naval Defence Act (1889) was passed because of increased naval competition from France, Germany and Japan. It introduced the 'two-power standard', which required the Royal Navy to be as powerful as the next two biggest navies combined (which were at that time France and Russia). A major shipbuilding programme began and forced the resignation of British Prime Minister William Gladstone, who found himself isolated after resisting the idea.

By 1907, Britain had signed the *Entente Cordiale* with France, the Great Rapprochement with the USA, the Anglo-Japanese Alliance and the Anglo-Russian Entente, leaving the Royal Navy to focus on the threat of the Imperial German Navy.

The naval arms race during this period brought about the first naval submarines and the impressively modern dreadnought battleships, capable of being built in just over a year and therefore just the job for an arms race.

FAMOUS SHIPS

HM *Holland 1*

The Navy's first submarine was HM *Holland 1* (official designation: HM *Submarine Torpedo Boat No. 1*), launched at Barrow-in-Furness in 1901, the same year in which the Submarine Service was formed. She was less than 20 metres long and petrol-driven, with a crew of eight and an armament of three torpedoes to fire from her one torpedo tube.

After sinking off the Devon coast on her way to the scrapyard in 1913, she was recovered in 1982 and has been displayed at the Submarine Museum in Gosport since 1983. In 2001, her centenary year, the Royal Mail put a photo of her on the 65p stamp.

FAMOUS SHIPS

HMS *Dreadnought*

Named after a ship of the line at the Battle of Trafalgar, HMS *Dreadnought* was the fastest and best-armed battleship on the seas when she was launched in 1906. As the first battleship driven by steam turbines and with a speed of almost 22 knots, she made other battleships look out of date. Her ten 12-inch guns, with a range of 17,990 yards (10.22 miles) and a capacity to fire two rounds a minute, made everything else look like the cannons of yesteryear. As we will see, she went on to become the only battleship in history to sink a submarine.

She also gave her name to a revolution in naval warfare, as 'dreadnought' became the generic term for a generation of battleships around the world.

⚓ *FAMOUS SAILORS* ⚓

ADMIRAL 'JACKY' FISHER
(1841–1920)

John Arbuthnot 'Jacky' Fisher was one of the most celebrated officers in the history of the Navy. He was actively involved for over sixty years, having started his career during the Crimean War and ending it during World War One. From a comparatively poor background, he made friends in the right places and forged his way up through the ranks, becoming a gunnery expert along the way. He was not well liked by everyone, surrounding himself with like-minded officers who became known as the 'fish pond', but there was no doubting that he was at the forefront of technological innovation.

His reforms over a twenty-year period ranged far and wide and included the introduction of the dreadnought battleship, which ensured the Navy's dominance in World War One. Fisher also made time to found the Navy's torpedo unit, rewrite the naval training manuals and improve communication methods – he is even credited with being the first to use 'OMG' (in a letter to Churchill) as an abbreviation for 'Oh, My God!' and can therefore also be considered the founder of modern textspeak. LOL.

IN OTHER NEWS

Not everything the Navy did in the early twentieth century was in preparation for a war that looked increasingly likely with each passing year. Some officers remained concentrated on expanding the glory of the British Empire through exploration – none more so than Robert Falcon Scott, who was becoming increasingly obsessed with claiming the South Pole for Britain.

⚓ FAMOUS SAILORS ⚓

SCOTT OF THE ANTARCTIC
(1868–1912)

Robert Falcon Scott joined the Navy as a cadet at the ripe old age of thirteen and worked his way through the ranks to captain in a career that took him to South Africa, the Caribbean and, of course, Antarctica.

The British National Antarctic Expedition (1901–04), later known as the Discovery Expedition after the name of his ship, took place under the naval command of Scott and was mostly staffed by Navy personnel. It led to the discovery of the Polar Plateau, so cold that it cannot sustain land animals or birds, not even penguins. Scott returned home to a hero's welcome and a job in Naval Intelligence.

He took command of his second Antarctic expedition in 1910, which later became known as the Terra Nova Expedition, again after the name of his ship. He reached the South Pole on 17 January 1912, only to find that Norwegian Roald Amundsen had beaten him to it by some five weeks. He and his party never made it back, freezing to death in the most inhospitable conditions known to man.

WORLD WAR ONE (1914–18)

I was a dealer in stocks and shares,
And you in butters and teas;
And we both abandoned our own affairs
And took to the dreadful seas.

RUDYARD KIPLING

World War One saw a huge increase in the Navy's manpower (from 250,000 to 450,000) and the birth of submarine and naval air operations. Although stretched thinly around the world to protect the British Empire, the primary objectives of the Navy's Grand Fleet of around 160 ships were to blockade Germany, to keep North Atlantic shipping lanes open and to counteract the submarine warfare practised by German U-boats.

The war was only thirty hours old when the small cruiser HMS *Amphion* was sunk with the loss of 130 men, two weeks before the first casualty suffered by the British Expeditionary Force on the embryonic Western Front. Whereas soldiers were much more likely to be wounded than killed during World War One, the opposite was true for sailors, given the very high mortality rate on exploding or sinking ships.

Many identifiable sea battles took place, the most notable of which was the Battle of Jutland in 1916, and lessons were learned from the failed Gallipoli Campaign in the Dardanelles, although even there the Submarine Service covered itself in glory. The Marines, as the major component of the Royal Naval Division, also saw significant action.

THE BATTLE OF HELIGOLAND BIGHT (1914)
The Battle of Heligoland Bight was the first naval engagement of the war, taking place in the North Sea and resulting in a morale-boosting British victory after ten German ships were sunk or badly damaged. For fear of further losses, Kaiser Wilhelm ordered the German High Seas Fleet to remain in port for several months thereafter. Within a month, though, a German U-boat had sunk the cruisers HMS *Aboukir*, *Hogue* and *Cressy* off the Netherlands, with the loss of 1,450 British sailors.

THE BATTLE OF THE FALKLANDS (1914)
After a German cruiser squadron commanded by Graf Maximilian von Spee had defeated the Navy's East Asia Squadron off the coast of Chile at the Battle of Coronel in November, the Admiralty sent a task force to track them down. The Germans suddenly appeared in the South Atlantic while the British ships were refuelling at Port Stanley in the Falkland Islands, but, seeing that the British could outgun him, von Spee sped off into the open seas. The British battlecruisers were faster, though, and soon caught up and destroyed the German squadron. Only 215 German sailors survived out of 2,086, with von Spee and his two sons amongst the dead.

THE BATTLE OF DOGGER BANK (1915)
The Battle of Dogger Bank was fought in the eponymous shipping forecast area of the North Sea after British cryptographers had intercepted and decoded messages that gave away the position of the German ships, which then turned tail in the face of the larger and faster British squadron. The battlecruiser SMS *Blücher*

was sunk and over a thousand Germans were killed or captured, with just fifteen British lives lost. Owing to poor signalling and targeting errors, though, the British ships were still outhit by the Germans three to one, resulting in heavy damage to HMS *Lion* and HMS *Tiger*.

THE GALLIPOLI CAMPAIGN (1915–16)

The main amphibious assault of the war took place in the Dardanelles strait in 1915, where British pre-dreadnought battleships, which were in any event too outdated to be used against the German High Seas Fleet, tried to force their way through to Constantinople (now Istanbul). This was an attempt to keep the sea route open to Russia, Britain's ally across the Black Sea.

They were undone, though, by the superior guns, mines and defensive positions of the Ottoman Empire (now Turkey), giving lie to the perception of the time that the Ottoman Empire was 'the sick man of Europe'. What had been conceived as a purely naval operation by the First Lord of the Admiralty, Winston Churchill, then resulted in forces being landed. Over 40,000 Allied troops were lost in the resulting campaign, with the only real successes being the evacuation of remaining land forces by sea and some effective submarine operations in the Sea of Marmara (more of which below).

FAMOUS SHIPS

HMS *M.33*

Built in just two months at the Harland and Wolff shipyard in Belfast in 1915, HMS *M.33* was a small Monitor-class warship that punched way above her weight as a shallow-draughted, floating gun platform designed to bombard coastal positions from the sea or from rivers.

She saw action when she supported the landing at Suvla during the Battle of Gallipoli in 1915, evacuated British troops from there in January 1916 and played a part in the capture of the Greek fleet at Salamis Bay later that year. Immediately after World War One she was deployed to the North Russian Expeditionary Force in Murmansk, where she covered the evacuation of British and White Russian forces during the Russian Civil War.

She later served as a mine-laying training ship in Portsmouth, where she remains today as a museum ship in Portsmouth Historic Dockyard.

GREAT SEA BATTLES
THE BATTLE OF JUTLAND (1916)

Fought just off the top of Denmark in the North Sea, the Battle of Jutland was the most significant naval engagement of World War One, and the most significant ever in terms of gun-armed battleships and battlecruisers. The German High Seas Fleet commanded by Vice Admiral Reinhard Scheer lined up against the Royal Navy's Grand Fleet under Admiral Sir John Jellicoe.

More than a hundred years on, opinion remains divided on who won the battle, but there is no doubt that the Germans inflicted the greater losses on account of their superior tactics, more effective armour-piercing shells and more modern communications (they used wireless signals as opposed to the ship-to-ship flag and lamp signals of yesteryear used by the Navy).

LOSSES SUSTAINED AT THE BATTLE OF JUTLAND

	Fleet size	Losses
British Grand Fleet	151 ships	6,784 seamen 14 ships: • 3 battlecruisers • 3 armoured cruisers • 8 destroyers
German High Seas Fleet	99 ships	3,039 seamen 11 ships: • 1 battlecruiser • 1 pre-dreadnought • 4 light cruisers • 5 destroyers

It was clearly a numerical victory for Germany against the odds, but more importantly it was a strategic victory for Britain because the Grand Fleet survived and kept control of the North Sea and the world's oceans generally throughout the war. The British blockade continued unabated, causing great hardship for the German people, and the Imperial German Navy knew from that point on that it didn't have the strength to compete for long in surface sea battles and concentrated instead on submarine warfare. As one New York newspaper put it at the time: 'The German Fleet has assaulted its jailor, but is still in jail.' ·

FOOTNOTES TO THE BATTLE OF JUTLAND

▶ When HMS *Invincible* exploded during the battle, she split in two and sank within ninety seconds. With only six survivors, 1,026 British sailors lost their lives, including Rear Admiral Horace Hood. Lady Hood, his widow, later sent individual letters of condolence to all those who were bereaved by the loss of the ship.

▶ The twenty-year-old Prince Albert, the future King George VI, was mentioned in despatches for his action as a turret officer aboard HMS *Collingwood* in the middle of the line.

⚓ FAMOUS SAILORS ⚓

BOY JACK CORNWELL
(1900–16)

HMS *Chester* was hit by seventeen German shells during the Battle of Jutland, but she did not go down. Amongst the thirty-five men who were killed or later died of their wounds was sixteen-year-old Jack Cornwell, the sight-setter on a 5.5-inch gun mounting. With the rest of his gun crew dead or mortally wounded, he remained at his post awaiting orders until the end of the battle, where he was found alive, but with shards of steel penetrating his chest. He died two days later, becoming a national symbol of bravery after the *Daily Sketch* ran his story.

Following his burial in a communal grave in Manor Park cemetery in Essex, the *Daily Sketch* campaigned for something more fitting. As a result, he was reburied with full naval honours in the same cemetery and posthumously awarded the Victoria Cross (VC) for his bravery. Funds raised by selling small flags and penny stamps bearing his image paid for a dedicated ward for disabled sailors at the Star and Garter Home for Disabled Ex-servicemen in Richmond, Surrey.

He remains commemorated today by the Cornwell Scout Badge (he was a Boy Scout at the time he joined the Navy in 1915 at the age of fifteen), which is awarded 'in respect of pre-eminently high character and devotion to duty, together with great courage and endurance'. Both the naval gun that was his post on HMS *Chester* and the VC he was awarded can be viewed in the Imperial War Museum in London.

BOYS WILL BE BOYS

At the ripe old age of fifteen, Jack Cornwell was not the youngest boy to join up during World War One. Private Denis Robert Kearns joined the RMLI (Royal Marines Light Infantry) in 1914 aged fourteen years three days and disembarked in France aged fourteen years 194 days. The youngest recruit, though, was Gunner Walter James Taylor, who joined the RMA (Royal Marines Artillery) in 1917 aged just thirteen years 150 days.

ROOM 40

The British codebreakers in World War One became known as 'Room 40' because that was the room in the Old Admiralty Building in London that they were assigned to work from. The team was initially formed of teachers and other staff from the naval colleges at Osborne, Dartmouth and Greenwich, but they were so successful that they intercepted and deciphered around 15,000 German intelligence signals during the war.

The most important interception was the telegram sent by the German Foreign Minister Arthur Zimmermann to the German ambassador in Mexico in January 1917. It promised Mexico the US states of Arizona, New Mexico and Texas if Mexico joined the war on the side of Germany, and its interception was a significant reason for the USA entering the war on the side of the Allies, which proved to be the beginning of the end for German hopes of victory.

Room 40 was merged in 1919 with the Army's Intelligence Unit to form the Government Code and Cypher School, housed at Bletchley Park during World War Two and later becoming Government Communications Headquarters (GCHQ) in Cheltenham.

⚓ FAMOUS SAILORS ⚓

ADMIRAL JOHN JELLICOE
(1859–1935)

One of the officers from Jacky Fisher's 'fish pond', John Jellicoe commanded a rifle company of the Naval Brigade in the Anglo-Egyptian War of 1882 and saw further action with the brigade in the Boxer Rebellion of 1900, where he confounded a field doctor and a chaplain by not dying of serious battle wounds. He recovered and become a gunnery expert as he rose through the ranks.

In 1914, Winston Churchill, as First Lord of the Admiralty, gave Jellicoe command of the Grand Fleet. During the complex Battle of Jutland in 1916, it fell to him to control the movements of 150 ships, but his visibility was often limited by fog or by the smoke that bellowed from damaged warships, and he was further hampered by insufficient communication from around the fleet and from his Commander-in-Chief, David Beatty, in particular. As Churchill put it, Jellicoe was the only man who could have lost the war in an afternoon, but he didn't, and history would go on to record Jutland as the battle that ultimately won the war.

Promoted to First Sea Lord later that year, Jellicoe tried to ensure that lessons were learned from Jutland. He revised the Grand Fleet Battle Orders, the Navy's 'rule book', to allow subordinate officers greater levels of initiative during action and to offer guidance for night fighting.

⚓ FAMOUS SAILORS ⚓

ADMIRAL DAVID BEATTY
(1871–1936)

David Beatty led a successful gunboat attack in the Anglo-Sudan War and, like Jellicoe, recovered from wounds received during the Boxer Rebellion in China, where he helped to relieve the Naval Brigade. Rising rapidly through the ranks, he went on to fight in most of the major engagements of World War One, including as Commander of the Battlecruiser Fleet at the Battle of Jutland. Many historians portray him as a charismatic and courageous leader, while others see him as a somewhat gung-ho, egocentric commander who sometimes lost sight of the bigger picture and could have done more to keep Jellicoe informed of developments at Jutland (an ITV documentary in 2016 lent credence to the belief that he falsified records and put pressure on the author of the battle analysis to hide his failings).

Taking over from Jellicoe, Beatty was made Commander-in-Chief of the Grand Fleet in 1916 and maintained control of the North Sea for the rest of the war. Having received the surrender of the German High Seas Fleet at the end of the war, he went on to hold the post of First Sea Lord for an unprecedented period of eight years.

As tensions mounted between Britain and the emerging power of the USA after World War One, Beatty was instrumental as a negotiator of the Washington Treaty of 1922, which agreed to equal numbers of battleships, battlecruisers and aircraft carriers for both countries.

SCAPA FLOW

Scapa Flow in the Orkneys was so heavily fortified as the base of the Navy's Grand Fleet during World War One that only two U-boats attempted to enter the harbour. Both were sunk on sight. The terms of the armistice after the war required Germany to surrender its High Seas Fleet to the Royal Navy, which they duly did in the Firth of Forth, following which they were escorted to Scapa Flow. Rather than see their seventy-four ships distributed amongst the victorious Allies, however, the skeleton German crews scuttled their own fleet there in 1919, sinking fifty-four vessels before the British could intervene.

SUBMARINE WARFARE

The fledgling Submarine Service operated in the Baltic Sea, proving its worth in the successful 1915–16 blockade of Germany and providing two of the very few successes of the Gallipoli Campaign by decimating the Ottoman fleet in the Sea of Marmara and closing off the Dardanelles to German U-boats.

They also did what they could to protect merchant ships crossing the Atlantic with vital supplies for Britain and its allies. This was a particularly difficult task during the periods that Germany practised unrestricted submarine warfare, which meant that merchant as well as naval vessels were attacked without warning, as with the sinking of the Cunard liner *Lusitania* in May 1915. German U-boats were so successful that they sank up to thirteen vessels a day, leaving Britain with just two weeks' food supply at one point.

The anti-submarine measures employed by the Navy included mines, depth charges, torpedoes, barrier nets and hydrophones (underwater microphones able to detect the sounds of enemy submarines). They also used Q-ships, which were merchant vessels with hidden weapons to lure submarines into surface attacks, whereupon the Q-ships would reveal their weapons and open fire. In the end, though, the only really effective tactic was to send the merchant ships in convoys protected by the surface and submarine fleets.

One unusual success came when the battleship HMS *Dreadnought* rammed and sank the German U-boat SM *U-29*, the ship's revolutionary Krupp cemented armour allowing her to cut the U-boat in two. She remains the only battleship in history to have achieved the feat of sinking a submarine.

THE CONTRIBUTION OF THE LOCH NESS MONSTER IN WORLD WAR ONE

One of the U-boats sunk by the Navy during World War One, SM *UB-85*, was discovered in 2016 by marine engineers laying power cables under the Irish Sea off Stranraer in Scotland. This revived a legend that the U-boat had been unable to dive after being attacked by a sea monster in 1918, thereby allowing a Navy patrol boat to sink her. The legend arose from stories told by the rescued crew of the sunken vessel, who were reportedly unable to believe what their eyes had seen. That crew probably didn't know what the Navy knew: that the Loch Ness Monster has to pass right by Stranraer on her way home from her holidays in the warmer waters of the Mediterranean.

THE ROYAL NAVAL AIR SERVICE (RNAS)

The RNAS was formed in 1914 and started out with just ninety-three aircraft, six airships, two balloons, twelve coastal stations and around 700 personnel, but it was soon leading the way in the development of aviation and the integration of aircraft into its fleet of ships. By the end of the war, it had 2,949 aircraft, 103 airships,

126 coastal stations and 55,000 personnel, and air support was considered a must for all the world's navies.

The first purpose-built aircraft carrier, HMS *Argus*, was not launched until 1918, so the RNAS had to make do with seaplanes and aircraft that could be carried on ships converted for this function. Many of the aeroplanes that took off from a ship's deck could not reland on it, so their pilots either had to find a friendly shore or ditch themselves in the sea close to their mother ship after they had completed their operations.

The RNAS also supplied crack fighter squadrons to the Western Front and took part in the earliest, somewhat speculative bombing campaigns. Flight Sub Lieutenant Reginald Warneford did succeed in destroying a Zeppelin by dropping bombs on it in 1915, for which he became the first Royal Navy pilot to receive the VC, only to die in an air crash a few days later.

Sopwith Pups, Triplanes and Camels were some of the iconic aeroplanes used for reconnaissance, patrol and combat purposes by RNAS pilots, three of whom are even today considered pioneers of aviation.

▶ John Alcock attacked three German aircraft in his Sopwith Camel, forcing two of them into the sea, before going on to pilot the first transatlantic flight just after the war.

▶ Squadron Commander Edwin Dunning became the first person to land an aircraft on a moving ship when he landed his Sopwith Pup on HMS *Furious* in Scapa Flow in 1917, but the third time he tried it he was killed when the plane veered off the starboard bow. The lessons learned from his bravery revolutionised naval warfare, and the Dunning Cup is still awarded annually to the officer considered to have done most to further aviation in connection with the fleet.

▶ One of the junior officers of the RNAS was Marine Engineer Barnes Wallis, who would go on to invent the bouncing bomb used in the Dambusters raid in the Ruhr Valley in World War Two.

FAMOUS SHIPS

HMS *Furious*

Launched in 1917, the light cruiser HMS *Furious* was a pioneering ship of naval aviation. Her size, speed and defensive capability (two 18-inch guns, the largest in the Navy at that time) made her a candidate to operate aircraft from, so in 1917 her forward gun was replaced with a take-off deck. Biplanes like the Sopwith Pup and the Short 184 floatplane took off from her successfully on a number of occasions, and her speed of 25–30 knots was what made it possible for Edwin Dunning to land a plane on a ship for the first time.

She was rebuilt between 1922 and 1925 with a full flight deck and saw further action during World War Two, ferrying naval and RAF aircraft around Europe and West Africa and attacking German ships whenever she got the chance.

In April 1918, the RNAS amalgamated with the Royal Flying Corps as the Royal Air Force, but would re-emerge as the Fleet Air Arm (FAA), initially under the umbrella of the RAF and then back under Admiralty control at the beginning of World War Two.

The RNAS Armoured Car Section

The RNAS surprisingly provided Britain's first-ever mechanised land forces in 1914, using Rolls-Royce and Mercedes cars to pick up stranded airmen. Their commander, Charles Samson, then hit upon the idea of arming the vehicles with Maxim guns and having them boiler-plated by shipbuilders. The Army became so excited at this development that by the following year they had snaffled the vehicles for their Machine Gun Corps. It was also the Navy who led the way on tank development for the Western Front, because the Landships Committee responsible for the initiative was instigated by Winston Churchill as First Lord of the Admiralty and was composed mainly of naval officers and engineers.

The Royal Naval Division (RND)

The RND was an infantry division of three brigades formed at the start of the war. One brigade was formed with men from the Royal Marine Light Infantry and Royal Marine Artillery; the other two consisted of around 20,000 Navy and Marine reservists and volunteers not needed at sea. It went on to achieve a lot for a makeshift division.

- ▶ The division saw action at the Siege of Antwerp in 1914, having arrived there in requisitioned London buses and with their ammunition in their pockets. Six thousand sailors held off 60,000 German soldiers for six days.

- ▶ At Gallipoli, RND Marines were sent ashore to assess the damage to Turkish fortifications following bombardment by British and French warships and to complete the destruction where possible. They were also the last to leave Gallipoli, once they had provided cover for the withdrawal of British, ANZAC and French troops from the beach.

- ▶ On the Western Front, the 63rd (Royal Naval) Division fought as part of the British Army, seeing action at Ancre (a British attack at the Battle of the Somme), Arras (where they captured the village of Gavrelle and took 679 German prisoners), Ypres and Passchendaele.

- ▶ During the night raids on Zeebrugge and Ostend in 1918 to block the canals that led to U-boat pens, around two hundred marines of 4th Battalion were sent ashore to destroy German gun positions. They were cut down when the wind changed direction and blew away the smokescreen and heavy gun support they had been promised, resulting in a casualty rate of almost fifty per cent.

The accomplished war poet Rupert Brooke was a junior officer with the division, fighting at Antwerp in 1915 and dying from an infected mosquito bite en route to Gallipoli the following year, but it turned out he wasn't the only poet in the division.

The Battle of Codson's Beard

Because the RND was commanded by the Army on the Western Front, there was much tension between Navy tradition and strict Army discipline. This came to a head when Major General Cameron Shute held an inspection during a lull at the Battle of the Somme and ordered some naval soldiers to shave off the beards which they had previously been given 'leave to grow'. One Sub Lieutenant Codson was having none of it and appealed to higher naval authority, who overturned Shute's order. Serving in the battalion at the time was poet A. P. Herbert, who encapsulated the incident beautifully in his poem 'The Battle of Codson's Beard', which he finished off as follows:

> *And now, when the thin lines bulge*
> *and sag, and man goes down to man,*
> *A great black beard like a pirate's*
> *flag flies ever in the van;*
> *And I've fought in many a warmish spot,*
> *where death was the least men feared,*
> *But I never knew anything quite so hot as*
> *the Battle of Codson's Beard.*

WORLD WAR TWO (1939-45)

The Battle of the Atlantic was the determining factor all through the war. Never for one moment could we forget that everything happening elsewhere, on land, at sea or in the air, depended ultimately on its outcome.

WINSTON CHURCHILL

A naval arms race had gathered pace in the years leading up to World War Two. At the outbreak of the war the Royal Navy remained the largest in the world, with 134,000 personnel, around 1,400 vessels and another 123 at various stages of construction or commissioning. These included four new Illustrious-class aircraft carriers and five new King George V-class battleships. It would end the war with 865,000 personnel, having lost 51,000 in battle, and more than 4,800 ships, second only to the US Navy in size.

The Navy was the only one of the British Armed Forces continually in action throughout World War Two. Without it, there would have been no successful evacuation of Dunkirk, no damage inflicted upon the Italian Navy at Taranto, no successful Malta or Arctic Convoys, no foundations for victory laid in the Battle of the Atlantic and no successful Normandy landings. Without those successes, there may have been no liberation of Europe and the British Pacific Fleet may never have set sail for Japan.

HMS *Warspite* and other capital ships (the term used for the Navy's most important warships) made headlines for all the right reasons; HMS *Hood* for the wrong reason entirely. Andrew Cunningham and Bertram Ramsay added their names to the long list of great British admirals; the Marines became the specialists in arriving by sea to fight on land; and the Fleet Air Arm came to prominence. Submarine warfare became increasingly significant, while anti-submarine warfare became crucial, given the huge numbers of U-boats deployed by Germany.

THE BATTLE OF THE RIVER PLATE (1939)

The Battle of the River Plate was the first naval engagement of World War Two. Because the German pocket battleship *Admiral Graf Spee* had been sinking merchant ships off the coast of South America, three British cruisers hunted her down in the River Plate estuary and inflicted damage to her fuel system, although not before she had scored hits on all three of the British ships and inflicted severe damage on HMS *Exeter* in particular.

The German captain sought refuge and repairs for his ship in the neutral port of Montevideo, but while there he decided to scuttle his ship rather than face any Allied warships that might be waiting for him in the River Plate when the permitted seventy-two hours in a neutral port were up. Not least because the British had fooled the Germans into believing that a large fleet awaited the *Admiral Graf Spee* should she choose to sail, Adolf Hitler was not best pleased with the decision of the ship's captain, Hans Langsdorff, who committed suicide shortly afterwards in Buenos Aires.

NAVAL BATTLES OF NARVIK (1940)

The naval Battles of Narvik in 1940 were part of the Allied response to the German invasion of Norway and were fought in the freezing waters of the Ofotfjord. Although successful, the Allies lacked the capability to follow up on land after they had destroyed the German invasion fleet, which meant that Germany continued to occupy the country.

One chance encounter took place between the destroyer HMS *Glowworm* and the German cruiser *Admiral Hipper*. After being badly damaged by artillery fire from the much larger German ship, the *Glowworm* attempted to torpedo her anyway and rammed her in the process. The *Admiral Hipper* survived the encounter, but the *Glowworm* sank shortly afterwards. Her captain, Lieutenant Commander Gerard Broadmead Roope, was awarded a posthumous VC, the first VC to be awarded in World War Two.

By the time the Allies withdrew from Norway three months later (its relative importance had diminished following the fall of France and the Low Countries), the Germans had lost three cruisers, four submarines and ten destroyers, which put paid to any chances they might have had of later taking control of the English Channel. However, the Allies themselves had lost two cruisers, six submarines, nine destroyers and an aircraft carrier, so the Norwegian Campaign was not seen at home as a success. It cost Neville Chamberlain his job as British prime minister and led to his replacement by Winston Churchill, who, ironically, had been the driving force behind the campaign as First Lord of the Admiralty. It was seen by many as a repeat of his failed Gallipoli Campaign twenty-four years earlier.

⚓ PATRICK DALZEL-JOB ⚓
(1913–2003)

Patrick Dalzel-Job was a Naval Intelligence Officer and Royal Marine Commando during World War Two. An accomplished linguist, sailor, navigator, parachutist, diver and skier who knew Ian Fleming (who also served in Naval Intelligence before taking up writing), he has inevitably been portrayed as one of the real-life action men that inspired the fictional James Bond. Dalzel-Job even had the rebellious streak required of James Bond, having disobeyed an order to stop the civilian evacuation of Narvik in 1940 after the Allied troops had been successfully removed. He saved around 5,000 Norwegians from German reprisals, for which King Haakon of Norway awarded him the Knight's Cross of St Olav, thereby preventing his court martial at the hands of the Admiralty.

He went on to lead commando raids in Norway, carry out operations in Special Service midget submarines and destroy specific targets in German-held territory during Operation OVERLORD, having pushed on from Utah Beach with the Royal Marine Commandos assigned to help him. His court martial would arguably have been somewhat short-sighted.

THE EVACUATION OF DUNKIRK (1940)

Operation DYNAMO was the evacuation of Allied troops from the beaches and harbour at Dunkirk, necessitated by the rapid progress of the German Army through northern France and the Low Countries. It lasted for eight days between 26 May and 4 June 1940.

Constantly hampered by German air attacks and sea torpedoes, the Navy ferried the stranded troops back to England in destroyers, minesweepers, gunboats, torpedo boats and anything else they could get their hands on. They were aided by merchant ships, ferryboats, fishing boats, lifeboats and even pleasure craft, all manned by volunteers who had responded to the government's call for help. A huge flotilla of little boats ferried men out to the larger vessels and some of these small craft are still in use and proudly belong to the Association of Dunkirk Little Ships.

By 4 June, 338,226 troops had been safely evacuated to fight another day, although the Navy lost six destroyers and around 7,000 men in the process.

FAMOUS SHIPS

HMS *Hood*

Launched in 1920, the 'Mighty Hood', as she became known, was the largest warship in the world and a potent symbol of British imperial strength between the wars. Her Empire Cruise of 1923–24 took her to South Africa, India, Australia, New Zealand, Canada, the USA and many other colonies and dependencies. The fuel bill alone was horrendous, given her fuel consumption of 9 feet to the gallon, but the peoples of the British Empire flocked to see her, and the pomp and ceremony that accompanied her wherever she went announced to the rest of the world: 'If you want to pick a fight with us, this is what you'll be up against.'

She was out of date by the start of World War Two, though. Her firepower remained impressive enough, as evidenced when she took part in the destruction of the French fleet at Mers-el-Kébir off French Algeria in 1940 to prevent it from falling into German hands, but she was vulnerable to being hit on her unarmoured deck. Unfortunately, that is exactly what happened in 1941 in the Denmark strait when shells fired from the German battleship *Bismarck* from a distance of 10 miles caused her to explode and sink within 5 minutes. Even though the *Bismarck* itself was sunk a few days later, the sinking of the Mighty Hood was a huge blow to British morale at the time. It remains the Navy's largest warship to have been lost and, with only three of her 1,418 crew surviving, its greatest loss of life from a single ship.

OPERATION FISH

In June and July 1940, the Navy was charged with moving the wealth of the British nation across the North Atlantic to Canada. It was a particularly risky time to do so, with forty per cent of all Allied ships in the North Atlantic having been sunk by U-boats in May 1940. Over 1,500 tonnes of gold plus the nation's stocks and securities were successfully moved in twelve ships from Greenock on the River Clyde to Halifax, Nova Scotia, and on by train to Montreal and Ottawa. The stocks and securities filled the bottom three floors of the Sun Life Building in Montreal and the gold filled the basement of the Bank of Canada in Ottawa. The stocks, securities and gold were converted into cash to run the war effort, in particular by buying war goods from the USA, and it was planned that Churchill would run the Commonwealth from Montreal in the event of Britain being invaded by Germany.

GREAT SEA BATTLES
THE BATTLE OF THE ATLANTIC (1939–45)

The Battle of the Atlantic was the longest campaign of World War Two. It was also the longest and most complex naval battle in history, and the outcome of the war depended on it. Churchill described it as the one conflict that kept him awake at night.

The struggle to prevent German U-boats, warships and aircraft from sinking the merchant ships that brought essential food, weapons and supplies across the Atlantic was exhausting, and victory came at a heavy price. The ships and submarines of the Navy and the aircraft of the RAF and FAA attacked U-boats at every opportunity, but still the latter succeeded in sinking thousands of merchant vessels – 956 of them in 1942 alone. The battle eventually turned in the Allies' favour for a number of reasons.

▶ U-boat movements could be tracked following the all-important breaking of the German Enigma code at Bletchley Park in 1940 and the seizure of a complete Enigma machine after three convoy escort ships captured a U-boat in 1941.

▶ Detection of U-boats improved with revolutionary radar and direction-finding techniques.

▶ The Navy received a bonus of around fifty second-hand US Navy destroyers in exchange for providing the Americans with some strategic overseas bases.

▶ The introduction of ahead-throwing anti-submarine weapons proved more effective than dropping depth charges over the sides of warships.

▶ The introduction of the Leigh Light on RAF patrol bombers illuminated U-boats while they were recharging their batteries on the surface at night, making them easier targets.

▶ The mid-Atlantic air gap was finally closed in 1943 once aircraft development achieved the longer ranges required.

▶ The Admiralty moved Western Approaches Command from Plymouth to Liverpool to be nearer to the convoys.

▶ The Allies remained committed to escorting the Arctic Convoys to Soviet ports, which kept Stalin on board and tied up a large part of Germany's naval and air forces. A crucial victory was secured at the Battle of the North Cape off Norway in December 1943, when the German battleship *Scharnhorst*, previously responsible for the sinking of several Allied convoy escort ships, was finally lured into battle and sunk.

▶ The USA entered the war and, after initially rejecting the idea of convoys, for which they suffered unnecessary losses, they eventually got with the convoy programme.

By the end of the war, 3,500 Allied merchant ships and 175 warships had been sunk in the Atlantic, with 72,200 Allied naval and merchant seamen losing their lives. Germany lost 783 U-boats and around 30,000 sailors. Over a hundred convoy battles and around a thousand ship-to-ship encounters had taken place over thousands of square miles of ocean. Once the Allies had finally gained the upper hand, though, it paved the way for convoys to bring more and more troops and materials from the USA and opened up the possibility of an Allied invasion of Europe.

⚓ FAMOUS SAILORS ⚓

CAPTAIN 'JOHNNIE' WALKER
(1896–1944)

Captain Frederic John Walker, known affectionately as Johnnie Walker after the whisky of that name, was the most successful anti-submarine warfare commander of World War Two. Rescued from early retirement by the outbreak of war, he was mentioned in despatches for the part he played in the evacuation of Dunkirk and then given command of the 36th Escort Group based at Liverpool.

In his first major engagement in December 1941, his group sank four U-boats, including one which was depth-charged and rammed by Walker's own ship. It was the first significant convoy victory for the Allies and Walker was awarded the Distinguished Service Order (DSO) for his efforts.

He went on to sink more U-boats in the Battle of the Atlantic than any other Allied commander, with 25.5 U-boat kills to his name (the half was shared with the RAF). His was the greatest single contribution to ultimate victory in the battle that the Allies could least afford to lose.

In July 1944, he died of a cerebral thrombosis, attributed to overwork and exhaustion.

THE BATTLE OF THE MEDITERRANEAN
(1940-45)

The Battle of the Mediterranean was fought between the Italian Navy (Regia Marina), supported by German U-boats and the Luftwaffe, and the Royal Navy, supported by other Allied warships. The prizes at stake were the supply lines to their respective armies and airbases in North Africa and southern Europe. The Italian fleet greatly outnumbered the Navy's Mediterranean Fleet, which therefore concentrated its efforts on holding the three key strategic points of Gibraltar, Malta and, at the top of the Suez Canal, Alexandria.

The Battle of Calabria (1940)

The first pitched battle of the Mediterranean saw the two sides line up in equal numbers when their respective supply convoys bumped into each other off the toe of Italy. Their paths had crossed because the Allies had been on their way to Malta from Alexandria at the same time as the Italians happened to be sailing from Naples to their North African base at Tripoli. The engagement ended in a draw, with three ships damaged on either side and both convoys heading on to their destinations after the battle.

The Battle of Taranto (1940)

The Navy's surprise attack on the Italian fleet at anchor in Taranto was designed to reduce the Italian threat to the Malta Convoys. It didn't just take the Italians by surprise, though – it took the world by surprise, as it was the first time that carrier-borne aircraft had ever attacked a heavily armed fleet (see also p.98). It succeeded in reducing Mussolini's naval capability for a while, but the Italian Navy was strong enough to carry on regardless.

The Battle of Cape Matapan (1941)

In order to pre-empt an Italian naval strike on a convoy supplying the British Expeditionary Force in Greece, the Allies sank two Italian destroyers and three heavy cruisers. The decisive factors had been the interception of Italian signals at Bletchley Park (which was how the Allies knew what to expect) and the absence of radar on the unsuspecting Italian ships as the Allies closed in on them.

The Evacuation of Crete (1941)

When it had become clear that Greek and other Allied forces from Britain, Australia and New Zealand were trapped along with Cretan civilians on the south of the island following a German airborne invasion, the Navy managed to evacuate about half of the 40,000 or so Allied troops before the remainder were captured or killed.

The Siege of Malta and the Malta Convoys (1940–42)

The strategic importance of British Malta between Sicily and North Africa was not lost on either side, and for a while it looked as if the Axis powers of Germany and Italy might starve the island into submission. Several Allied convoys were decimated, preventing essential supplies from reaching the island, and regular air attacks and bombardments from the sea left it further weakened. Notwithstanding those reversals, though, the Allies held on to ensure Malta's survival, with the following successes making the difference.

- ▶ The annihilation of a convoy taking supplies to the Italian Army and Germany's Afrikakorps in Libya (the Duisburg Convoy, 1941).

- ▶ The destruction of a convoy taking aviation fuel to Libya (the Battle of Cape Bon, Tunisia, 1941).

- ▶ The delivery of aviation fuel to Malta in August 1942 on board SS *Ohio*, an American tanker with a British crew. It was part of Operation PEDESTAL, which suffered the loss of nine out of fourteen Allied merchant vessels plus four Navy warships, but the aviation fuel rejuvenated the air offensive against Axis shipping in the Mediterranean and allowed air cover for the arrival of more fighter planes by sea (the planes completed the journey themselves, by flying to the island from the aircraft carriers that had brought them from Britain).

▶ Tipped off by the codebreakers at Bletchley Park, the Allies used Malta as a base to disrupt Axis supplies to North Africa ahead of the Second Battle of El Alamein in October 1942. Victory against the undersupplied Axis powers at El Alamein finally lifted the Siege of Malta, leaving the island free to serve as Allied Advance HQ for the invasion of Sicily the following year.

The courage and resilience of the Maltese people throughout the long siege later resulted in the island being awarded the George Cross.

⚓ FAMOUS SAILORS ⚓

ADMIRAL ANDREW CUNNINGHAM
(1883–1963)

Andrew Browne Cunningham was known widely by his nickname 'ABC'. Having seen action in the Naval Brigade during the Second Boer War, he went on to command a destroyer during World War One, being awarded the Distinguished Service Order (DSO) for his actions in the Dardanelles. As Commander-in-Chief, Mediterranean Fleet during World War Two, he led the victories at the Battles of Taranto and Cape Matapan and the evacuation of Crete, and he controlled the crucial Mediterranean supply lines between Gibraltar,

Malta and Alexandria. He commanded the invasion of French North Africa in 1942, and in 1943 he oversaw the naval contribution to the invasion of Sicily and the surrender of the Italian fleet off Malta.

He was promoted to First Sea Lord at the end of 1943, in which position he contributed to the strategies employed for the Normandy landings and the deployment of a British Pacific Fleet in 1944.

He is arguably best remembered for the following three reasons.

► Following the victory he masterminded at Taranto, he declared that the battle should be remembered for 'having shown once and for all that in the Fleet Air Arm the Navy has its most devastating weapon'.

► In order to disguise British intentions before the Battle of Cape Matapan, he arranged a game of golf and a fictitious evening reception in Alexandria within earshot of enemy agents, before boarding HMS *Warspite* under cover of darkness. His subterfuge paid off handsomely when the Italian Navy was taken by surprise in Cape Matapan off Thessaloníki the next day.

► Without any air cover against Luftwaffe dive-bombers, he refused to let the British Army down during the evacuation of Crete. He sacrificed nine warships and 1,828 Navy personnel to rescue around 16,500 British Army troops who were otherwise at the mercy of the advancing Germans. He famously and defiantly said: 'It takes three years to build a ship; it takes three centuries to build a tradition.'

OPERATION NEPTUNE

Operation NEPTUNE was the naval contribution to the invasion of Normandy. On D-Day, 6 June 1944, it set in motion the largest armada in history, which had gathered together from all over the United Kingdom off the southern tip of the Isle of Wight. The gathering point was officially designated Area Z, but it was quickly nicknamed Piccadilly Circus. Around seven thousand vessels set off from there for the beaches of Normandy, making their way through recently swept minefields as RAF bombers and airborne troops went ahead.

By the end of D-Day, 132,815 troops had been landed from around 6,000 warships and landing craft on to the five beaches of Sword, Juno, Gold, Omaha and Utah. It was the beginning of Operation OVERLORD, the liberation of Western Europe, which would ultimately turn the war in the Allies' favour. By the time Operation NEPTUNE concluded on 30 June, convoys across the English Channel had delivered 861,838 troops, 157,633 vehicles and 501,834 tonnes of supplies. Much of this was made possible through the ingenuity of Corncobs (five false harbours created by the scuttling of large ships) and Mulberry Harbours (ninety-five concrete floating pontoons that allowed vehicles to exit directly from ship to shore). The remains of two Mulberry Harbours can still be seen at Portland Harbour in Dorset and Langstone Harbour in Hampshire.

SOUTHWICK HOUSE

In 1943 Southwick House to the north of Portsmouth was chosen as Supreme Headquarters, Allied Expeditionary Force while the Normandy landings were being planned. As D-Day approached, the house was cordoned off from the rest of HMS Dryad, the Royal Naval Navigation School that had been moved there after Portsmouth Harbour had been bombed. The toy manufacturer Chad Valley was commissioned to supply the large plywood wall map of the English Channel that can still be seen in the house today. To maintain secrecy, the two carpenters who erected and joined together the pieces of the map were required to remain in Southwick House until the invasion got underway.

During this time, Southwick House and the sleepy village of nearby Southwick played host to George VI, Winston Churchill, Field Marshal Montgomery, General Eisenhower, Admiral Bertram Ramsay and Naval Lieutenant Prince Philip, who showed the Queen his favourite wartime pub, the Golden Lion, when they visited Southwick in 1973. Southwick House, still as HMS Dryad, served as the Navy's Maritime Warfare School from 1945 until 2004.

⚓ FAMOUS SAILORS ⚓

ADMIRAL BERTRAM RAMSAY
(1883–1945)

Having been coaxed out of retirement by Winston Churchill at the start of the war, Bertram Ramsay was the Navy's foremost expert in amphibious warfare during World War Two. He oversaw Operation DYNAMO (the successful evacuation of Dunkirk in 1940) from tunnels underneath Dover Castle. Because of the overwhelming success of the operation, he was invited to report personally on the evacuation to George VI.

He planned the successful amphibious invasion of French North Africa in April 1942, thereby adding much-needed impetus to the North African Campaign that would lead to the Axis powers being driven out of Africa by the following year.

As Naval Officer Commanding, Eastern Task Force, he prepared the amphibious landings required to invade Sicily in 1943. The invasion achieved its strategic goals to drive Axis air, land and naval forces from Sicily and reopen Mediterranean shipping lanes. The invasion of Italy could get underway and Mussolini would be toppled from power as a result.

As Allied Naval Commander-in-Chief, Expeditionary Force, he then had responsibility for the greatest invasion of all, Operation NEPTUNE. He planned the Normandy landings from Southwick House, and it was there that he decided that 5, 6 or 7 June, subject to weather conditions, would be the date for D-Day.

FAMOUS SHIPS

HMS *Warspite*

Launched in 1915, the battleship HMS *Warspite* served her country with distinction in both world wars. She belonged to the Queen Elizabeth class, the first oil-fired British battleships, which were capable of 23 knots. Their strength came from a combination of speed, effective armour protection and firepower, housing eight 15-inch guns with each shell weighing 1,938 pounds (879 kilograms), the same as a Fiat 500.

Warspite survived incredible punishment at the Battle of Jutland in 1916, being holed a staggering 150 times. Her armour protected her crew well, with only fourteen killed out of more than a thousand on board.

Extensively modernised between 1934 and 1937, she went on to gain more battle honours (fourteen) than any other ship in World War Two, and the most battle honours ever awarded in total to an individual ship in the Navy (fifteen), earning her the nickname the 'Grand Old Lady'.

The action she saw during World War Two included the following notable contributions.

▶ Atlantic and Mediterranean convoy duties.

▶ Firing one of the longest gunnery hits from a moving ship on a moving target in history, when she hit the Italian battleship *Giulio Cesare* from a distance of about 15 miles.

▶ Providing cover for the air strike on Taranto.

▶ Bombarding Italian coastal batteries to facilitate the invasion of Italy from North Africa.

▶ Firing the first shot from the sea on D-Day and going on to provide cover for landings on three separate beaches (Sword, Utah and Gold).

▶ Living up to her name by surviving a ramming and numerous hits from shells, bombs, mines and a guided missile.

THE BRITISH PACIFIC FLEET

The British Pacific Fleet formed in late 1944 was the largest-ever foreign deployment of the Navy. A task force of carriers, submarines and support vessels so far from home had to learn new skills to supply ships at sea and fight the enemy with a strong emphasis on naval air power – twelve aircraft carriers supplied a total of 750 aircraft.

Bases were established at Sydney and Manus Island, Papua New Guinea. Manus, the largest of the appropriately named Admiralty Islands, was dubbed 'Scapa Flow with palm trees' and was an ideal position from which to attack the Japanese.

Kamikaze attacks were a constant threat and damaged several carriers, but their armoured flight decks, which their US Navy counterparts did not have, withstood the blows to the extent that they were back operating in no time.

When HMS *King George V* bombarded naval installations near Tokyo, it was the last time that a British battleship ever fired in action (because battleships would be replaced by aircraft carriers and cruisers as the capital ships of the Navy after World War Two).

THE SUBMARINE SERVICE

The Submarine Service saw three significant areas of operation during World War Two: the North Sea, the Mediterranean and the waters of the Far East.

THE NORTH SEA

After the German Army invaded Norway in 1940, British submarines were deployed to attack their supply ships and lay minefields in the North Sea. Outnumbered from that point on by German U-boats and up against the constant threat of German anti-submarine warships and aircraft during long daylight hours, thirty-four Allied submarines were lost in the North Sea during the war. However, they did play their part in inhibiting German supply routes and they did have some battle successes, including the sinking of an enemy U-boat, patrol ship and two cruisers.

CAT AND MOUSE

One British submarine in particular made a name for herself in the North Sea. HMS *Venturer*, having already sunk five merchant ships and one surfaced U-boat since entering service in August 1943, went after German U-boat *U-864* in Norwegian waters in February 1945. *U-864* had been waiting for a shipping escort to Japan to deliver jet-engine parts and 65 tonnes of mercury for use in explosives, so *Venturer* gave chase while the U-boat remained unprotected. After playing cat and mouse while *U-864* zigzagged ahead, Lieutenant Jimmy Launders anticipated the next turn that *U-864* would make and released four torpedoes towards the course he predicted for her. It took four minutes for the torpedoes to get there and the fourth one scored a direct hit, splitting *U-864* in two. It remains the only occasion in wartime that one submarine has intentionally sunk another while both were submerged.

THE MEDITERRANEAN

The Tenth Submarine Flotilla, known as 'the Fighting Tenth', operated out of Malta from 1940 onwards, initially using fifteen T-class or older submarines. Torpedoes were in short supply so they had to choose their targets carefully, but they had some successes. HMS *Truant* alone destroyed one Italian submarine, nine merchant vessels and a motor torpedo boat. Losses were heavy, though, because the submarines were too visible and therefore vulnerable from the air, and many losses also occurred from mines. Eleven of the fifteen submarines were lost in the first year.

When the new, smaller, more manoeuvrable U-class submarines arrived in 1941, the submarine offensive gained some momentum. The star of the show was HMS *Upholder*, sinking three U-boats, a destroyer and fifteen transport ships before being sunk herself in 1942. Her commanding officer, Lieutenant Commander Malcolm Wanklyn, was heralded as a 'submarine ace' and was awarded the VC for sinking the heavily defended Italian liner SS *Conte Rosso*.

By sinking a great many merchant ships throughout the Battle of the Mediterranean, the Submarine Service prevented a huge tonnage of Axis supplies reaching North Africa.

THE FAR EAST

In 1944, the Eastern Fleet of the Submarine Service sank the Japanese cruiser *Kuma*, three submarines, six smaller naval vessels and 41,000 tonnes of merchant shipping. British submarines also landed and supplied Special Forces troops, rescued airmen from the ocean and shelled Japanese shore installations.

By March 1945 they had control of the Strait of Malacca, preventing any further supplies travelling by sea to Japanese forces in Burma, and in June 1945 the ageing T-class submarine HMS *Trenchant* sank the Japanese heavy cruiser *Ashigara* in the Java Sea, hitting her with five out of eight torpedoes fired from a distance of more than 2 miles.

MIDGETS AND CHARIOTS

Midget submarines and Chariots were designed to reach the areas that conventional submarines couldn't get into and required a great deal of bravery on the part of those who undertook the dangerous operations they were allocated.

Midget submarines

Midget submarines, known as X-craft, were towed by their mother ship to a position within 70 miles of their objective, after which a crew of four set off on their own, including the frogmen whose job it was to attach delayed-action explosives to their targets.

In September 1943, six X-craft were deployed to mine German battleships, which had been holed up in a Norwegian fjord, safe from conventional submarine attack. Two of them succeeded in mining the *Tirpitz*, putting it out of action for at least six months. VCs were awarded to two of the frogmen who carried out the raid. X-craft were later used as navigational beacons for amphibious tanks on the Normandy beaches on D-Day.

In the Pacific, the improved XE-class was deployed to carry out a daring underwater raid in Singapore Harbour, using limpet mines to cripple the Japanese cruiser *Takao*, with further VCs being awarded to two of those who took part. In another raid, they succeeded in cutting the seabed communication cables that linked Japanese-occupied Saigon with Singapore and Hong Kong.

Chariots

Chariots were the size and shape of a torpedo and piloted by frogmen sitting astride them, hence they came to be known as 'human torpedoes'. The charioteers had to wear a closed breathing suit, nicknamed the 'Clammy Death', so that no bubbles would be released on the surface. When they arrived at their target, they removed the warhead from the front of the Chariot and attached it as a limpet mine.

In January 1943 Navy frogmen guided their Chariots into Palermo Harbour and succeeded in damaging two Italian vessels. In October 1944 two Chariots entered Phuket Harbour in Thailand and successfully mined two Italian liners. Sixteen Navy frogmen lost their lives in Chariot operations during the war and twenty earned medals for their courageous acts.

THE ROYAL MARINES (RM)

In addition to their traditional role of supplying naval gunners, the Marines during World War Two developed into the amphibious commando forces they are now famous for being the world over.

They saw action, and they made a difference, around the globe. Nine RM Commando battalions (numbered 40–48) were created during the war, each of them assigned to one of four Combined Services Commando Brigades. Five of the battalions played their part in the liberation of Europe; two saw action largely in Italy, Yugoslavia and Greece; and two fought in South East Asia.

EUROPE

- ► A small raiding party of marines was first ashore near the Norwegian harbour town of Namsos in April 1940, seizing the approaches in preparation for the landing of the British Army.

- ► At the Battle of Crete in 1941, a composite battalion of marines fought a rearguard action under heavy air attack to assist the evacuation of Allied troops from the island.

- ► Disembarking on Gold Beach during the Normandy landings, 47 Commando had been assigned the primary objective of capturing Port-en-Bessin, which was earmarked as the main fuel-delivery point for the Allies until Cherbourg could be captured. Having sustained heavy losses after five of their landing craft hit mines on the way in to the beach, they dug in for the night and completed their mission over the next two days after some intense fighting.

- ► As part of the Combined Services 30 Assault Unit, 41 Commando took part in the Normandy landings and succeeded in their appointed task of taking out a German radar station. The unit later fought its way into Cherbourg and other ports before capturing the German naval base at Bremen the following year.

- ► Landing on Juno Beach on D-Day, 48 Commando spearheaded the assault on Langrune-sur-Mer, which was liberated after heavy fighting and losses. They held their position while vital reinforcements and equipment were brought ashore.

▶ In November 1944, 41, 47 and 48 Commando Battalions took part in the decisive Battle of the Scheldt, which finally silenced German coastal batteries at Walcheren. This was key to Allied use of the deep-water port at Antwerp to support the liberation of Europe.

▶ At Lake Comacchio in Italy in 1945, Corporal Thomas Peck Hunter single-handedly cleared a farmhouse containing three enemy machine guns, firing a Bren gun from his hip. He lost his life while drawing fire as his troop took cover. He was the tenth and most recent marine at the time of writing to be awarded the VC.

AFRICA

▶ In May 1942, fifty marines were landed at a Vichy French naval base on Madagascar because a British Army assault was being held up by heavy fire from the shore. The marines captured two of the shore batteries, leading to the quick surrender of the French.

▶ In November 1942, during the North Africa landings of Operation TORCH, the Special Intelligence Unit (which included men of the Royal Marines and Royal Navy and later became Combined Services 30 Assault Unit) occupied Italian naval headquarters near Algiers and seized German and Italian battle orders and code books.

SOUTH EAST ASIA

▶ After the battleship HMS *Prince of Wales* and the battlecruiser HMS *Repulse* had been sunk by Japanese aircraft in 1942, the Marine detachments that were rescued from them amalgamated with the Army's Argyll and Sutherland Highlanders to fight on as the Plymouth Argylls. They sustained heavy losses during the intensive fighting that led to the Fall of Singapore, not least because of their determination to evacuate civilians from Singapore to Sumatra. Some of those captured ended up working on the infamous Burma Railway.

▶ In January 1945, 42 and 43 Commando Battalions took part in the decisive Battle of Hill 170 in Burma that broke the Japanese supply and retreat route to and from Rangoon.

ROYAL MARINE PILOTS IN THE FAA
A total of eighteen RM officers led FAA squadrons during the war, including fighter ace Ronald Cuthbert Hay, who flew in the Norwegian campaign, the evacuation of Dunkirk, the Battle of Britain and the Far East. His total kills were four solo and nine shared.

THE COCKLESHELL HEROES
Under the command of Major 'Blondie' Haslar, Operation FRANKTON was carried out in 1942 by the Royal Marine Boom Patrol Detachment. A call had gone out for volunteers who were 'eager to engage the enemy, indifferent to personal safety and free of strong family ties'. Thirty-four men applied and twelve set off for the operation following a period of training on the River Thames.

The objective was to canoe 70 miles up the River Gironde to Bordeaux and use limpet mines to sink cargo ships preparing to take German equipment to Japan. Of the six two-man canoes transported by the submarine HMS *Tuna* to the Gironde estuary, one was damaged trying to leave the submarine, two capsized in rough waters and one sank. The two that made it succeeded in damaging four ships in the harbour.

Of the ten men who successfully launched from the submarine, only Major Haslar and his canoe partner Bill Sparks made it home, having escaped over the Pyrenees with the help of the French Resistance and then making their way down through Spain to Gibraltar. Two of the commandos drowned and the other six were captured and shot, including the other two who had successfully completed the operation alongside Haslar and Sparks.

The raiding party used the Cockle Mark II canoe, hence the name of the 1955 film that made the raid famous: *Cockleshell Heroes*.

⚓ FAMOUS SAILORS ⚓

LIEUTENANT COLONEL 'BLONDIE' HASLAR
(1914–87)

In addition to commanding Operation FRANKTON, 'Blondie' Haslar also received an OBE and the Croix de Guerre for the operational support he gave to the French Foreign Legion in the Norwegian Campaign of 1940. Later he trained special forces to fight the Japanese in Burma and he is said to have despatched a total of 173 raids against the enemy throughout the course of the war. He was responsible for many of the warfare concepts that led to the formation of the Special Boat Service (SBS).

After the war, he became a great single-handed yachtsman, personally inventing a self-steering gear for yachts and instigating the first Single-handed Transatlantic Race, in which he came second to Francis Chichester, who sailed a much larger boat.

THE FLEET AIR ARM

Progress in naval aviation had faltered under the command of the RAF between the wars, leaving the FAA to start World War Two with just 232 aircraft, many of which were unsuitable for modern warfare. It finished the war with over 3,000 aircraft, operating around the world from eighty-three naval air stations and fifty-one aircraft carriers, which had by then replaced battleships as the capital ships of the fleet. They flew fighters, torpedo bombers and reconnaissance aircraft and made a significant contribution to the war effort.

THE BATTLE OF THE RIVER PLATE (1939)
A Fairey Seafox seaplane launched from HMS *Ajax* 'spotted' the shells fired at the *Admiral Graf Spee* from the Navy's warships so that their subsequent salvos could become increasingly accurate. The pilot who flew the mission, Lieutenant Lewin, became the first FAA officer to be decorated in the war when he received the Distinguished Service Cross (DSC) for his part in the action.

NORWAY (1940)
Lieutenant Commander William Lucy led the formation of sixteen Blackburn Skuas that bombed and sank the German light cruiser *Königsberg* in Bergen Harbour in April 1940. He shot down at least

five planes himself, making him one of the first Allied fighter aces of the war.

At the Battle of Narvik in June, a U-boat was sunk by a float-equipped Fairey Swordfish catapulted from HMS *Furious*. It was the first U-boat to be sunk in World War Two and the only one to have been sunk by an aircraft launched from a battleship. The Swordfish crew on HMS *Warspite* contributed by providing the only air cover to the Allied Expeditionary Force ashore.

THE EVACUATION OF DUNKIRK (1940)
Ten Fairey Albacores and nine Blackburn Skuas bombed pontoon bridges over the border in Belgium to slow down the advance of the German Army on Dunkirk. Two Skuas were lost to Messerschmitts on the way back, but they also took down a Messerschmitt in return.

THE BATTLE OF BRITAIN (1940)
The FAA supplied aircrew to bolster RAF fighter squadrons during the Battle of Britain, as well as loaning two entire Naval Air Squadrons (804 and 808 NAS) to RAF Fighter Command, with the Sea Gladiators of 804 NAS assigned to defend dockyards.

THE BATTLE OF CALABRIA (1940)
Fairey Swordfish planes launched from HMS *Eagle* torpedoed and sank the Italian destroyer *Leone Pancaldo* at the end of the Battle of Calabria.

THE BATTLE OF TARANTO (1940)
The FAA's attack on the Italian fleet at Taranto in south-east Italy was one of the most daring actions of World War Two. Taking off from HMS *Illustrious*, the two-man crews of twenty-one almost obsolete Fairey Swordfish biplanes faced heavy anti-aircraft artillery and nearly two hundred machine guns while dropping their aerial torpedoes and bombs on the naval port. They had undertaken the mission anticipating a loss rate of fifty per cent, but just two aircraft were lost. The Swordfish scored hits on three battleships, one heavy

cruiser, two destroyers and two aircraft on the ground, also causing severe damage to the port itself. The daring raid revolutionised naval warfare and was used by the Japanese the following year as a blueprint for their own attack on the US Navy fleet at Pearl Harbor.

As Churchill put it at the time: 'By this single stroke the balance of naval power in the Mediterranean was decisively altered.'

THE BATTLE OF THE ATLANTIC (1939-45)

The FAA hunted and attacked U-boats during the Battle of the Atlantic, using Fairey Swordfish and Grumman Martlets. A crisis point was reached in 1942 as U-boats operated freely in the mid-Atlantic air gap that was out of range of shore-based aircraft at the time. Flight decks were quickly built on top of the hulls of merchant ships, allowing the FAA to at least provide a degree of start-to-finish protection to Allied convoys from the sea.

THE SINKING OF THE *BISMARCK* (1941)

After Churchill instructed the Navy to sink the *Bismarck* after it had sunk HMS *Hood*, it took just two days for the Fairey Swordfish planes launched from HMS *Ark Royal* to torpedo her and jam her rudder, leaving her unable to avoid the surface ships that finished her off.

MALTA AND NORTH AFRICA (1940-42)

After their crews had perfected the technique of night-time torpedo bombing using airborne radar, the Fairey Swordfish and Albacores based at Malta destroyed 400,000 tonnes of enemy shipping, a crippling blow to Rommel's campaign in North Africa. Two Swordfish squadrons also acted as pathfinders over the North African desert, illuminating targets for the RAF bombers who followed behind.

THE BATTLE OF CAPE MATAPAN (1940)

At the Battle of Cape Matapan, Fairey Albacore and Swordfish bombers from HMS *Formidable* struck two Italian destroyers, a heavy cruiser and the battleship *Vittorio Veneto*, while a Fairey Fulmar shot down a German Junkers Ju 88 plane. The heavy cruiser and the two destroyers were later finished off by Navy ships.

THE CHANNEL DASH (1942)

After six Fairey Swordfish of 825 NAS took off from RAF Manston to intercept German battlecruisers and destroyers returning to Germany via the English Channel, they came up against intense anti-aircraft fire and attacks from enemy escort planes. They carried on regardless, but all six aircraft were shot down and only five of the eighteen aircrew survived. For his gallantry against overwhelming odds, their commanding officer, Eugene Esmonde, was posthumously awarded the VC.

SALERNO (1943)

The FAA used Supermarine Seafires (the naval equivalent of the Spitfire) off HMS *Formidable* and *Illustrious* to cover the support of Allied landing forces on mainland Italy. As land-based fighters were out of range at the time, the FAA squadrons flew a total of 713 sorties over 42 daylight hours.

THE NORMANDY LANDINGS (1944)

The FAA contribution to Operation NEPTUNE was significant, with Grumman Hellcat, Wildcat and Avenger aircraft providing air cover and carrying out day and night patrols to look for enemy U-boats, E-boats (German fast-attack vessels), midget submarines and even flying bombs, two of which were destroyed in mid-air by Avengers. Five of the FAA squadrons also 'spotted' for the naval guns of the fleet against shore and ship targets, correcting the fall of shot and identifying new targets.

In addition, several Avenger squadrons operated day and night with Coastal Command in Kent and Cornwall to protect the English Channel at both ends from German ships and U-boats.

THE PACIFIC THEATRE (1944-45)

FAA squadrons supplied seven different types of aircraft and flew over 7,000 operational sorties in the fight against Japan in the Pacific. Their contributions included the bombing of the oil refineries on Sumatra, the airfields of Sakishima Islands (to facilitate the US invasion of nearby Okinawa), the Japanese escort carrier *Kaiyo* and Tokyo itself. They also provided air cover for Allied ships against Japanese attacks, both conventional and kamikaze.

The attack on the Sumatran refineries was the largest operation ever carried out by a stand-alone FAA force, with the Grumman Avenger bombers of four different squadrons escorted by Hellcat, Corsair and Fairey Firefly fighters. They lost forty-eight aircraft, but destroyed sixty-eight Japanese planes in return – thirty in dogfights and thirty-eight on the ground. The bombing raid succeeded in cutting off Japanese access to much-needed fuel.

In one of the last bombing raids of the war, the Canadian pilot, Lieutenant Robert Hampton Grey, became the second FAA pilot to receive the VC in World War Two. He was killed attacking a Japanese destroyer, but not before flying in low enough to hit the destroyer while his plane was already in flames and being subjected to further heavy fire.

In the very last fighter combat of the war on 15 August 1945, the Seafires, Avengers and Fireflies that provided air cover against kamikaze attacks on the carrier HMS *Indefatigable* shot down eight Japanese aircraft for a single loss of their own.

INTO THE AGE
OF NATO AND
NUCLEAR POWER

The post-war years saw a rapid decline in the British Empire and a reduced appetite for military spending in the face of economic hardship at home. The Navy got smaller and the US Navy took over as the world's self-appointed policeman. The formation of the United Nations and NATO demanded a still significant naval contribution from the UK, though, and the Cold War was a constant reminder of the Soviet threat and the need to match nuclear threat with nuclear deterrent.

The second half of the twentieth century was not exactly without incident, however, and the 1982 Falklands Conflict in particular was a timely reminder of the need to maintain a UK expeditionary force capability.

The eventual collapse of the Soviet Union brought with it a new, broader focus on world events. Terrorism has become the scourge of the modern world and the need for military intervention has kept minds focused on the need for a modern Navy capable of responding to modern threats.

THE YANGTZE INCIDENT (1949)

The frigate HMS *Amethyst*, en route from Shanghai to Nanking to serve as guard ship for the British embassy there during the Chinese Civil War, was seriously damaged on 20 April 1949 when she came under fire from Chinese Communist Forces (the People's Liberation Army) on the northern bank of the Yangtze River. She ran aground for a while, which allowed the crew to evacuate twenty-two dead and thirty-one wounded, including their mortally wounded captain.

The remaining crew of sixty were stranded on board for the next three months, pinned down by sniper fire and low on provisions for much of the time. Attempts to free her by other Navy warships failed and resulted in further loss of life. Finally, on 30 July, she slipped away downriver after dark, using a passenger ship as cover. The passenger ship was sunk by gun batteries but the *Amethyst* made good her escape and rejoined the fleet the next morning, after which she was escorted to Hong Kong for repairs. A personal congratulatory message was received from King George VI, including a specific instruction to 'splice the main brace'. In 1957 the story was turned into a film called *Yangtze Incident* starring Richard Todd.

NAVY SPEAK
SPLICE THE MAIN BRACE

'Splice the main brace' is Navy speak for giving sailors an alcoholic drink for a job well done. It reflects the fact that one of the hardest jobs on board a sailing ship was an emergency repair to the main brace, the rope that is used to rotate a yard around the mast to allow the ship to sail at different angles to the wind. If the main brace was damaged in battle, it could not be repaired with a knot because it would not then be able to run through its blocks. Instead, it had to be spliced, meaning that the strands of the two broken ends had to be unravelled and then intertwined. The men who completed this difficult task, often under battle conditions, were given an additional tot of rum for their efforts, resulting in the term 'splice the main brace' becoming a euphemism for a well-earned or celebratory drink. Today, the main brace is also spliced on a change of monarch or to celebrate a royal wedding or baby.

THE KOREAN WAR (1952)

The Navy deployed a fleet of warships, plus five different aircraft carriers at one time or another, to assist the UN task force throughout the Korean War, primarily to enforce a naval blockade in accordance with a UN resolution against North Korea after it had invaded South Korea. In one operation, the cruiser HMS *Jamaica* and the frigate HMS *Black Swan* joined with USS *Juneau* in sinking four North Korean torpedo boats and two mortar gunboats.

The FAA carried out sorties from the aircraft carriers with Supermarine Spitfires, Hawker Sea Furies and Fairey Fireflies, and also used the Westland Dragonfly helicopter in Search and Rescue missions for the first time. (See 'Famous Pilots' in the 'Fleet Air Arm' chapter to learn how a propeller-driven Sea Fury was used to shoot down a Chinese MiG jet.)

THE COLD WAR (1947-91)

In the face of the Soviet threat that prevailed from the 1950s onwards, an injection of military spending allowed the Navy to increase its capability from its post-war low. By the 1960s, it had the most powerful carrier fleet outside of the USA, along with a large fleet of frigates and destroyers and its first nuclear-deterrent submarines.

The Navy also augmented its anti-submarine capability with three Invincible-class carriers (HMS *Invincible*, HMS *Illustrious* and HMS *Ark Royal*) in the 1980s. The Sea King helicopters they carried were designed with anti-submarine warfare in mind.

In line with NATO policy, the Navy focused much of its anti-submarine capability on guarding the GIUK gap, which consists of two naval choke points – one between Greenland and Iceland, the other between Iceland and the UK (hence the acronym GIUK). In the event of the Cold War turning hot, Soviet submarines would have needed to pass through one of these two choke points, or the even narrower English Channel, to get to the North Atlantic.

THE COD WARS
The Navy sent warships to protect British fishing trawlers during the three Cod Wars (1958–61, 1972–73 and 1975–76) that were fought between the UK and Iceland. Each of the wars resulted in a British climbdown and an extension of the Icelandic exclusive fishing zone, because all Iceland had to do in the end was threaten to withdraw from NATO, which would in turn have afforded the Soviet Union access to the GIUK gap.

REACTING TO THE WORLD'S PROBLEMS
The Navy continued to play a significant global role during the second half of the twentieth century. Here are just some of the trouble spots in which it found itself in action.

- ▶ **Kuwait:** The Navy was called in to ward off an Iraqi invasion of Kuwait just after Britain gave Kuwait its independence in 1961. A rapidly deployed task force of carriers, destroyers and frigates put Iraq right off the idea. The battalions deployed with the task force included 42 and 45 Commando.

- ▶ **Tanganyika:** Not long after gaining independence in 1961, Tanganyika's new president, Julius Nyerere, asked for help in putting down a mutiny of the 1st Tanganyika Rifles, formerly the King's African Rifles of the British Army. The Navy despatched aircraft carrier HMS *Centaur* from Aden and, upon arrival in Dar es Salaam, 45 Commando went ashore and quickly restored order.

▶ **Borneo:** From 1962 to 1966 a huge Combined Services task force joined with Australian and New Zealand forces to support the Malaysian government during their confrontation with Indonesian communists on the island of Borneo. The Navy element of the task force consisted of thirty-one ships (including five aircraft carriers), five submarines, two commando units, three commando helicopter squadrons and some SBS sections. The daring flying of the helicopter squadrons during that conflict earned the aircrew the coveted nickname of 'Junglies', which is still used today.

▶ **Rhodesia:** In accordance with UN sanctions against Rhodesia (1965–75), the Navy blockaded the supply of oil to Rhodesia through the port of Beira in Mozambique.

▶ **Northern Ireland:** The Northern Ireland Squadron was established during the Troubles (1968–98) to prevent the movement by sea of arms for paramilitaries. The depot ships HMS *Maidstone* and HMS *Hartland Point* were berthed in Belfast as troop barracks and prison accommodation. The Marines completed around seventy tours of duty on the ground.

▶ **Persian Gulf:** The Navy was deployed to protect British shipping in the Gulf throughout the Iran-Iraq War (1980–88).

▶ **Falkland Islands:** The Navy was deployed to deliver and support the British task force that responded to the Argentinian invasion in 1982 (see 'The Falklands Conflict' below).

▶ **Iraq:** The Navy fought in the Gulf War (1990–91) against Iraq, after Iraq did finally invade Kuwait in 1990. Lynx helicopters, operating from frigates and destroyers, caused extensive damage to the Iraqi Navy with the Sea Skua anti-ship guided missile. The Marines were involved in protecting Kurdish refugees from Iraqi persecution.

▶ **Kosovo:** In 1999, Sea King helicopters operating from HMS *Invincible* were NATO's eyes and ears during the blockade of ships trying to take oil to Montenegro, while the Marines saw action on the ground. Tomahawk cruise missiles were launched at Serbian targets from the submarine HMS *Splendid*.

NUCLEAR SUBMARINES

Once the USA had shown the way in 1955 with USS *Nautilus*, the world's first nuclear-powered submarine, Admiral Lord Mountbatten (as First Sea Lord) pushed hard for Britain to do likewise and even convinced the Americans to supply us with their latest nuclear propulsion system.

Whereas diesel-powered submarines had to come close to the surface regularly to replenish their batteries and air supply, nuclear-powered submarines do not. They also have enough energy to power through the water faster than most surface warships.

The next revolution arrived within just a few years, as nuclear-armed submarines began to provide a powerful deterrent to all-out war. They became the nuclear deterrent platform of choice because they could patrol the oceans unseen, whereas land-based or aircraft-borne missiles were more susceptible to reconnaissance and therefore more vulnerable to attack at any time.

HMS *Dreadnought*

Entering service in 1963, the main role of HMS *Dreadnought*, Britain's first nuclear-powered hunter-killer submarine, was to detect and if necessary destroy enemy submarines. Her range and power allowed her to travel at sustained high speed from Rosyth on the Firth of Forth to Singapore and back in 1967, completing 26,545 miles submerged and 4,640 miles on the surface. Her versatility was proven when she became the first British submarine to surface at the North Pole in 1971.

Because she could remain submerged for months as opposed to weeks, her crew were at least afforded more spacious accommodation, for the first time having their grots (bunks) separate from their mess areas.

HMS *Valiant*
The development of a British nuclear propulsion system by Rolls-Royce allowed HMS *Valiant* to enter service in 1966 as the first all-British nuclear-powered submarine. She saw service in the Falklands Conflict in 1982.

HMS *Resolution*
The strategic capability of the Navy was transformed when HMS *Resolution*, Britain's first nuclear-powered, nuclear-armed submarine, went on patrol in 1968. Armed with Polaris ballistic missiles, the Resolution class became known as 'bombers' because they replaced the RAF's bomber aircraft as Britain's nuclear deterrent. The Polaris was a solid-fuel rocket akin to those used in space exploration. Having been fired from its tubes with enough high-pressure steam to drive it to the surface and into the air, the rocket engine took over as it left the water, sending the 16-tonne missile into the stratosphere with a range of 2,500 miles to its chosen target. A single Resolution-class submarine carried more destructive potential than the total amount of explosives detonated by all sides throughout World War Two.

HMS *Resolution* completed sixty-nine patrols in total by the time she was decommissioned in 1994.

THE FALKLANDS CONFLICT (1982)
The Navy played the leading role in Operation CORPORATE, taking a task force 8,000 miles across the Atlantic to liberate the remote Falkland Islands after they had been invaded by Argentina. Once there, the surface warships provided artillery cover from the sea as and when required, and air power was deployed from the two aircraft carriers that had set sail with the task force. Other significant naval contributions to the recapture of the islands included the following.

▶ A small detachment of marines from HMS *Endurance*, the Navy's Antarctic ice patrol ship that happened to be in the Falklands at the time of the Argentinian invasion, recaptured South Georgia before the task force even arrived.

▶ The Submarine Service went ahead of the main task force to gather intelligence through surveillance.

▶ The nuclear-powered submarine HMS *Conqueror* sank the Argentinian cruiser ARA *General Belgrano* (more of which below).

▶ Numerous Royal Marine and Army deployments were landed ashore, including the landing of 3 Commando Brigade at San Carlos Water ahead of their famous yomp across East Falkland to Stanley, during which they covered 56 miles in three days, carrying 120-pound (56-kilogram) loads, and defeated the enemy in several sharp engagements.

▶ FAA Sea Harrier jump jets shot down twenty-three Argentinian attack jets using Sidewinder missiles in air-to-air combat for no loss of their own, despite the Sea Harriers being outnumbered four to one at the outset.

▶ The Argentinian submarine *Santa Fe* was damaged by depth charges from a Wessex, the first helicopter ever to engage a submarine in battle, and was finished off with air-to-surface missiles fired by two Wasp helicopters.

▶ Helicopters rescued casualties from the Royal Fleet Auxiliary (RFA) ships *Sir Galahad* and *Sir Tristram* after they had been hit from the air, and an SAS (Special Air Service) deployment was rescued by helicopter from South Georgia in very difficult weather conditions.

The naval task force despatched to the Falklands was considerable, as illustrated by the following list of naval vessels that went south.

- 2 x aircraft carriers

  - HMS *Hermes* (with twenty-two Sea King helicopters and sixteen Sea Harrier jump jets on board)

  - HMS *Invincible* (with ten Sea King helicopters and twelve Sea Harrier jump jets on board)

- 2 x amphibious assault ships (HMS *Fearless* and *Intrepid*)

- 8 x destroyers (including HMS *Sheffield*, later sunk by an Exocet air-to-surface missile, and HMS *Coventry*, later sunk by free-fall aircraft bombs)

- 15 x frigates (including HMS *Antelope* and *Ardent*, both sunk, and HMS *Argonaut* and *Plymouth*, both of which suffered major damage)

- 1 x ice patrol ship

- 2 x patrol vessels

- 6 x submarines

- 3 x survey vessels

- 5 x minesweepers

- 10 x RFA oil tankers

- 6 x RFA landing ships (including RFA *Sir Galahad*, which was sunk, and RFA *Sir Tristram*, which suffered major damage)

- ► 5 x RFA supply ships

- ► 1 x helicopter support ship

- ► 2 x tugs

In addition to those sixty-eight RN and RFA vessels, forty-six Merchant Navy ships were also requisitioned as STUFT (Ships Taken Up From Trade).

- ► 3 x cruise liners

  - ❖ SS *Canberra* (converted to troop ship and carried 3 Commando Brigade RM and the Army's Parachute Regiment to the Falklands)

  - ❖ RMS *Queen Elizabeth 2* (converted to troop carrier, with 650 Cunard crew volunteering to look after the 3,000 troops of the Army's 5 Brigade en route to the Falklands)

  - ❖ SS *Uganda* (converted to hospital ship after dropping off 315 cabin passengers and 940 schoolchildren on an educational cruise at Naples)

- ► 8 x roll-on roll-off ferries

- ► 5 x cargo ships (including *Atlantic Conveyor*, which was sunk along with ten helicopters and most of the tents meant for infantry shelter on shore)

- ► 7 x freighters

- ► 15 x tankers

- ► 8 x support ships (three tugs, one repair ship, one cable ship, one diving support ship, two oilfield vessels)

As befitted a conflict that had been predominantly led by the Naval Service, the Argentinian surrender was taken on board HMS *Intrepid*, the amphibious assault ship that had been used for the San Carlos landings and later to house Argentinian prisoners of war. The success of Operation CORPORATE emphasised the reach and capability of British maritime power at a time when its future was under threat from the politics and economics of the day.

The sinking of the *General Belgrano*

On 1 May 1982, the Navy submarine HMS *Conqueror* spotted the Argentinian cruiser ARA *General Belgrano* heading towards the British task force, resulting in the decision to attack her. On 2 May, HMS *Conqueror* sank the *General Belgrano* with two out of the three torpedoes it had fired at her. It was the only sinking to date of a surface ship by a nuclear-powered (not nuclear-armed) submarine, and it was also the first time a submarine had fired a torpedo in action since World War Two. The Argentine Navy withdrew to its base and played no further part in the conflict.

DISASTER RELIEF AND HUMANITARIAN AID

The Navy has often been called in to help in remote areas only accessible by sea or where a heavy lift capacity is needed. Here is a short sample of the relief it has provided in times of great difficulty.

Ionian Islands, Greece: The cruisers HMS *Gambia* and *Bermuda* were quickly on the scene to provide emergency medical aid, food and water after Cephalonia and Zakynthos were all but destroyed by a series of earthquakes in 1953.

Montserrat: After the eruption of the Soufrière Hills volcano in 1995, the destroyer HMS *Liverpool* played a vital role in the evacuation of 7,000 people to Antigua and other Caribbean islands – impossible by aircraft at the time because the eruption had destroyed the airport.

Haiti: The landing ship RFA *Largs Bay* delivered over 600 tonnes of food and materials after a devastating earthquake in Haiti in 2010.

Philippines: The destroyer HMS *Daring* was in the Pacific when Typhoon Haiyan hit the Philippines in 2013 and was quickly on the scene to help devastated remote island communities. The carrier HMS *Illustrious* was in the Gulf at the time and sped 5,000 miles to deliver aid by helicopter, having picked up supplies in Singapore en route.

Sierra Leone: The casualty receiving ship RFA *Argus* was sent to Sierra Leone to provide aviation support and medical aid in the UK-led effort against the Ebola virus in 2014.

INTO THE TWENTY-FIRST CENTURY

The twenty-first century has seen no let-up in the troubles of the world, and the Navy has already seen significant action in some far-flung places.

Sierra Leone: The UK deployed a naval force led by the aircraft carrier HMS *Illustrious* to Sierra Leone in 2000. The marines of 42 Commando helped prevent the country's capital, Freetown, falling into rebel hands, thereby playing an important part in ending the country's long-running civil war.

Afghanistan: The marines of 40 Commando were the first troops into Afghanistan in 2000 and the last ones out twelve years later. Navy personnel deployed to the land-locked country included logistics officers, surgeons, nurses, bomb-disposal experts, and helicopter pilots and handlers.

Iraq: During the Iraq War of 2003 onwards, Navy ships bombarded shore targets to support the landing of marines on the Al-Faw peninsula, and submarines launched Tomahawk cruise missiles at specific land targets inside Iraq.

Libya: In 2011, a total of fourteen warships, submarines and RFA vessels supported combat, embargo and humanitarian operations to protect Libyan civilians from the Gaddafi regime. The following Navy contributions at that time illustrate vividly its capacity and capability to deploy an impressively rapid and joined-up amphibious operation.

The submarine HMS *Triumph* launched Tomahawk cruise missiles at land-based targets.

- ▶ The helicopter carrier HMS *Ocean* controlled the strike missions of Army Air Corps Apache attack helicopters and the surveillance flights of the Sea King helicopters of 857 Naval Air Squadron.

- ▶ Using her sophisticated air-surveillance technology, the destroyer HMS *Liverpool* controlled fourteen types of NATO aircraft for over 280 hours to ensure continuous coverage of the no-fly zone necessary to protect operations. *Liverpool* also bombarded onshore rocket batteries and other targets.

- ▶ The Mine Countermeasure Vessels HMS *Brocklesby* and *Bangor* cleared mines that threatened the flow of humanitarian aid and the evacuation of civilians.

- ▶ The tankers RFA *Wave Knight* and *Orangeleaf* kept Royal Navy and coalition warships fuelled off Libya for as long as required, while replenishment ship *Fort Rosalie* provided a shuttle service of stores and ammunition throughout.

- ▶ The frigate HMS *Cumberland* evacuated 454 civilians, including 129 British nationals, to Malta.

► The destroyer HMS *York* delivered medical and food supplies to aid agencies in Benghazi and evacuated forty-three people at risk.

If anyone ever tells you that the Navy lacks versatility, tell them about Libya in 2011.

⚓ **ADMIRAL SIR JONATHON BAND** ⚓
(1950–)

Jonathon Band joined the Navy as a junior officer in 1967 and worked his way up to the very top job of First Sea Lord by 2006. His early career included an exchange to the US Navy on board a guided missile cruiser, serving as Principal Warfare Officer on board the frigate HMS *Eskimo* and assuming command of the minesweeper HMS *Soberton*.

His later commands included the frigates HMS *Phoebe* and *Norfolk* and the aircraft carrier HMS *Illustrious*, which included a deployment to support UN and NATO operations during the Bosnian War. As Commander-in-Chief Fleet from 2002, he was involved in the planning of the Iraq War.

As First Sea Lord from 2006 to 2009, he pushed strongly for a modern, capable Navy that would serve the country for many years to come, including the two new supercarriers HMS *Queen Elizabeth* and *Prince of Wales*.

PART TWO

THE ORGANISATION AND ROLES OF THE MODERN NAVY

Si vis pacem, para bellum.
(If you wish for peace, prepare for war.)
THE MOTTO OF THE ROYAL NAVY

OVERVIEW

Her Majesty's Naval Service comprises the Royal Navy and the Royal Marines, although the shorthand 'Navy' is often used to describe the Service as a whole. The Naval Service is also known as the Senior Service, because it is the oldest of the British Armed Forces. Its primary role is naval, expeditionary and amphibious warfare, but its modern multifaceted role also includes peacekeeping, anti-piracy, counternarcotics, fishery protection, mine countermeasures, and humanitarian and disaster relief. It works with NATO and other countries and international organisations as necessary to fulfil its international obligations and to play its part in the enforcement of UN resolutions.

TOP MANAGEMENT

The overall management of the Naval Service is the responsibility of the Admiralty Board, chaired by the Secretary of State for Defence. It devolves the following responsibilities to the Navy Board, chaired by the First Sea Lord, who at the time of writing is Admiral Sir Philip Jones KCB.

- ▶ Delivery of naval capabilities.

- ▶ Maintaining the strategic (nuclear) deterrent.

- ▶ Naval planning and operations.

- ▶ Efficiency and morale throughout the Service.

- ▶ Provision of naval advice to the Permanent Joint Headquarters.

Navy Command HQ is at Whale Island, Portsmouth, and Commander Operations (Royal Navy) is the naval component of the Permanent Joint Headquarters (PJHQ) at Northwood in Hertfordshire. PJHQ commands joint and combined military operations and provides military advice to the MoD (Ministry of Defence). Joint operations involve components of the Navy, Army and RAF; combined operations involve working with the armed forces of other countries and with NATO.

THE STRUCTURE OF THE NAVY
The Navy today is made up of five arms.

- ▶ Surface Fleet

- ▶ Submarine Service

- ▶ Fleet Air Arm

- ▶ Royal Marines

- ▶ Royal Fleet Auxiliary

Those five arms are underpinned by the following services.

- Warfare Branch

- Engineering Branches (Weapon and Marine)

- Logistics Branch

- RN Police

- Royal Naval Reserve (RNR)

- Royal Marines Reserve (RMR)

- RN Medical Service

- Queen Alexandra's RN Nursing Service

- Chaplaincy Service

- Marine Services

We will look at each of the arms and services in the chapters that follow.

NAVAL SERVICE PERSONNEL

At the time of writing, the personnel figures for the Naval Service, as published by the MoD, were as follows:

- Trained regular strength: 29,500

- Royal Navy: 22,670; Royal Marines: 6,830

- Officers: 5,930; ratings: 23,570

- General Service (Surface Fleet): 20,830; Submarine Service: 4,050; Fleet Air Arm: 4,620

Notes:
Maritime Reserve strength (RNR plus RMR) was 3,480, giving a total trained strength of 32,980.

Twelve per cent of regular trained strength was female (officers and ratings).

3.5 per cent of regular trained strength was of ethnic minority origin (officers and ratings).

3,250 would-be officers and ratings remained in training at the time of writing, and therefore were not included in the trained regular strength figure.

The ranks of the Naval Service
The ranks of the Royal Navy and Royal Marines are quite different, because the Marines' ranks are more akin to those of the Army.

Royal Navy ranks
Commissioned officers of the Navy begin their careers by graduating from the officer training course at the Britannia Royal Naval College in Devon. They start out at the rank of midshipman, followed by automatic promotion to sub lieutenant after twelve months (while still training) and further automatic promotion to lieutenant after thirty months of satisfactory performance and once having moved into an operational environment. Further promotion up the ranks from that point is based entirely on merit.

Other ranks (ratings) undertake basic training at HMS Raleigh in Cornwall and start out as able rates. They can then rise through leading rate (or leading hand) to become a petty officer, the first of the senior rating ranks and also the first level of non-commissioned officer (NCO). Warrant officer is the highest rank that can be achieved as a rating. If good enough, a rating can also be selected for commissioned officer training.

Royal Marines ranks
Commissioned officers of the Royal Marines start at the rank of second lieutenant upon successful completion of officer training at

the Commando Training Centre in Devon. Enlisted Grades start at the rank of marine upon successful completion at that same training centre.

Here is the full list of the ranks of the Royal Navy and Royal Marines (with equivalent grades alongside each other where appropriate).

Royal Navy	Royal Marines
Officer Ranks	
Admiral	
Vice admiral	
Rear admiral	Major general
Commodore	Brigadier
Captain	Colonel
Commander	Lieutenant colonel
Lieutenant commander	Major
Lieutenant	Captain
Sub lieutenant	Lieutenant
Midshipman	Second lieutenant
Other Ranks	
Warrant officer	Warrant officer Class 1
	Warrant officer Class 2
Chief petty officer	Colour sergeant
Petty officer	Sergeant
Leading rate	Corporal
	Lance corporal
Able rate	Marine

THE FLEET

At the time of writing, the Navy had seventy-seven commissioned ships, nearly all of which were built in Britain (the one exception is the ice patrol ship HMS *Protector*, which was built in Norway). The breakdown of the ships is as follows.

Assault ships	3
Destroyers	6
Frigates	13
Patrol vessels	22
Ballistic missile submarines	4
Fleet submarines	7
Mine countermeasure vessels	15
Survey vessels	5
Historic warships	2

Note: The two 'historic warships' still in commission are HMS *Victory* and HMS *Bristol*. In addition to being a museum ship in Portsmouth Historic Dockyard, HMS *Victory* remains in commission as the flagship of the First Sea Lord. The destroyer HMS *Bristol* is retired from active service, which included deployment during the Falklands Conflict, but remains in commission as a training ship at the shore establishment HMS Excellent on Whale Island in Portsmouth Harbour.

HER MAJESTY'S NAVAL BASES (HMNB)

Today there are three naval bases in the UK, situated at Portsmouth in Hampshire, Devonport in Devon and Faslane in Scotland.

HMNB Portsmouth

There has been a permanent naval base at Portsmouth ever since King John ordered the building of a fortified wall around the natural harbour in 1212. Today HMNB Portsmouth employs around 17,000 people and is the home base of the Portsmouth Flotilla, which comprises:

- ▶ 6 x Type 45 destroyers

- ▶ 6 x Type 23 frigates

- ▶ 2nd Mine Countermeasures Squadron (eight vessels)

- ▶ Fishery Protection Squadron (three vessels)

- ▶ 1st Patrol Boat Squadron (fourteen vessels)

- ▶ Falkland Islands Patrol Vessel

- ▶ Gibraltar Squadron (two vessels)

- ▶ Fleet Diving Squadron

It will also be the home base of the two new aircraft carriers HMS *Queen Elizabeth* and *Prince of Wales*.

HMNB Devonport

There has been a Royal Navy dockyard at Devonport in Plymouth since 1691, and today HMNB Devonport is the largest naval base in Western Europe, with 4 miles of waterfront, fifteen dry docks, twenty-five tidal berths and five basins. Employing around 2,500 Naval Service and civilian personnel, it handles more than 5,000 annual ship movements. It is the home base of the Devonport Flotilla, which comprises:

- ▶ 3 x amphibious assault ships

- ▶ 7 x Type 23 frigates

- ▶ 4 x survey ships

- ▶ 1 x ice patrol ship

It is also home to Southern Diving Unit One; Flag Officer Sea Training for the Surface Fleet and Royal Fleet Auxiliary; and RM Tamar, the Amphibious Centre of Excellence for landing craft, small boats, engineering and assault navigation.

HMNB Clyde

Scotland's biggest single-site employer, with around 7,000 military and civilian personnel, HMNB Clyde is situated near Helensburgh in Faslane Bay at the top of Gareloch, from which position it enjoys easy access via the River Clyde to the North Atlantic. It is best known as the home of Britain's eleven nuclear submarines, four of which are armed with Trident missiles. In addition to the submarines, it is the base for the Faslane Patrol Boat Squadron (two vessels) and the 1st Mine Countermeasures Squadron (seven vessels). It is also home to the Northern Diving Group and Flag Officer Sea Training for the Submarine Service.

The Royal Naval Armaments Depot at Coulport 8 miles away is responsible for the storage and issue of all submarine-embarked weapons.

ROYAL NAVAL AIR STATIONS (RNAS)

The two principal airbases of the Royal Navy's Fleet Air Arm and its 174 aircraft are at RNAS Culdrose in Cornwall and RNAS Yeovilton in Somerset (more of which in 'The Fleet Air Arm' chapter).

OVERSEAS BASES

In addition to the permanent deployment of two patrol boats to the Port of Gibraltar, the Navy makes use of two overseas bases:

Falkland Islands: Mare Harbour on East Falkland is used as a deepwater port by RN ships patrolling the South Atlantic and Antarctica, and as a port facility and depot for the RAF airbase and British Army garrison established there following the Falklands Conflict.

Bahrain: A permanent Royal Navy base, known as HMS Juffair, has been re-established at the port of Mina Salman to support ships operating east of Suez (the site of the previous RN base there was taken over by the US Navy after Bahrain declared independence from the UK in 1971).

TRAINING ESTABLISHMENTS

As you might expect within an organisation that requires such an impressive range of skills, all of which need to be updated on a continual basis as technology and science continue to develop at an unrelenting pace, training is of the utmost importance to the Navy. The following are the key shore establishments responsible for delivering that training.

Britannia Royal Naval College

The Britannia Royal Naval College (BRNC) at Dartmouth in Devon, also known as HMS Dartmouth, is the Navy's officer training establishment. It provides initial officer training and ongoing leadership and diplomacy skills. The Navy has been training officers since 1905 on this impressive site (the architect was Sir George Aston Webb, whose other commissions included Admiralty Arch and the east front of Buckingham Palace), and before that on board the decommissioned wooden ships of the line HMS *Britannia* and *Hindostan* moored on the River Dart. Since 1990, courses have been integrated to absorb female naval officers.

Royal cadets in the past have included George V, George VI, the Duke of Edinburgh, the Prince of Wales and the Duke of York. Prince William also spent time at the college as part of his training with all three of the Armed Forces.

HMS Raleigh

HMS Raleigh is the shore establishment near Torpoint in Cornwall where all basic new-entry training for male and female ratings in the Navy takes place. The training ranges from learning the core values of the Navy (commitment, courage, discipline, respect, integrity and loyalty) to how to fire an SA-80 assault rifle and put out a fire at sea. In addition to the main site, there is a maritime training centre on the River Lynher (complete with decommissioned warship) and two remote bases for tough leadership and team-building exercises at Gutter Tor on Dartmoor and at Pier Cellars on the Rame peninsula.

As well as providing induction courses for new recruits, there are six specialist schools on site.

- ▶ **Military Training Unit:** Provides cutting-edge weapons training for sailors of all levels to ensure they can protect themselves and their teams while serving at sea or on land.

- ▶ **Board and Search Training School:** To prepare for the likes of counternarcotics or anti-piracy operations, practice boardings are carried out by day and night.

- ▶ **Defence Maritime Logistics School:** Specialist training for a range of logistics jobs at sea, including Logistics Officer (management of everything from operational supplies to humanitarian aid) and Supply Chain Specialist (worldwide delivery of vital stores and equipment).

- ▶ **Submarine School:** Training for specialists in weapons engineering and warfare for the Submarine Service.

- ▶ **School of Seamanship:** Teaching everything from basic safety at sea to advanced seamanship.

- ▶ **School of Maritime Survival:** Providing vital skills in firefighting, damage control, first aid and sea survival. All sailors (officers and ratings) must undertake this training before taking up an appointment at sea.

HMS Collingwood

HMS Collingwood, based at Fareham in Hampshire, is the lead establishment of the Maritime Warfare School (MWS), part of the Flag Officer Sea Training organisation, and home to the Maritime Warfare Centre (MWC), an independent unit responsible for Concept, Doctrine, Operational Analysis and Tactical Development in support of current operations. The MWC also runs some courses aimed at the higher levels of command.

As the Navy's largest training establishment, HMS Collingwood delivers the following elements.

- ► Advanced navigational skills, so that officers learn how to navigate ships from anywhere to anywhere else in the most challenging operational and meteorological conditions.

- ► Underwater warfare, teaching anti-submarine operations to those responsible for protecting individual ships, task forces or the nuclear deterrent.

- ► Engineering maintenance of the weapons and systems fitted to warships.

- ► Operational safety in the use of explosives, small arms and close-range combat.

- ► Use of ships' radar, sensors, and command and weapons systems to identify and engage threats and targets, including on the sea, under the sea and in the air.

- ► Principal Warfare Officer training to prepare Warfare Officers for the significant step up en route to Sea Command.

The MWS also delivers training at the following satellite sites.

▶ **Defence Diving School:** Basic military diving training to Navy and Army divers is given at Horsea Island, Portsmouth, with advanced training delivered at other sites on the south coast and in Scotland.

▶ **School of Hydrography and Meteorology, HMNB Devonport:** Provides training in the conducting and analysis of hydrographic surveys needed to support up-to-date nautical charting and military operations. It is possible to specialise in meteorology and oceanography, which are key elements of military planning because atmospheric conditions and the environmental properties of an ocean (e.g. its current) need to be factored in alongside the required charts. Military operations supported include anti-submarine warfare, mine countermeasures, amphibious assault and, in the case of meteorology, deployment of aircraft.

▶ **School of Nuclear, Biological and Chemical Defence:** Located at Whale Island, MWS elements of training include damage control and firefighting.

▶ **School of Physical Training, HMS Temeraire, Portsmouth:** Where PT Instructors learn to provide fitness regimes, coach and officiate in the twenty-three different sports practised in the Navy and provide opportunities for adventure training, including sailing, climbing and abseiling.

HMS Sultan

HMS Sultan at Gosport is home to the Defence School of Marine Engineering (DSMarE), the Royal Naval Air Engineering and Survival School (RNAESS) and the Nuclear Department. Their combined purpose is to supply the Navy with first-class engineering officers and ratings.

The DSMarE teaches surface ship and submarine marine engineering, from diagnostics to the operation and maintenance of the machinery used on board the Navy's vessels.

The RNAESS prepares Air Engineer Officers, Technicians and Survival Equipment ratings for operational duties and covers the whole range of aeronautical skills required to keep the Fleet Air Arm moving. The Nuclear Department provides training in naval nuclear propulsion and radiation protection, including hands-on experience on simulators of each of the Navy's in-class submarines.

HMS Sultan will close down in around 2026 as part of an ongoing consolidation of the Naval Estate, which is itself part of the ten-year Better Defence Estate project to reduce the footprint and improve the efficiency of the assets of the Armed Forces. Marine engineering training will relocate to HMS Collingwood in Fareham when the time comes.

Institute of Naval Medicine

The Institute of Naval Medicine in Gosport is home to the Navy's medical training, with extensive research, laboratory and clinical facilities available to all three of the Armed Forces, including during active military operations.

JOINT AND COMBINED MILITARY OPERATIONS

Whether working with the UK's two other Armed Forces or linking up with those of our allies, the Navy today must remain flexible enough to deploy within any wider force or exercise required for the job in hand.

Joint Warrior

Exercise Joint Warrior is a major training exercise held twice a year, involving thousands of Navy, Army and RAF personnel and utilising surface ships, submarines and aircraft. Fleet Operations in Northwood plan and coordinate the overall exercise, and the Faslane Naval Base serves as HQ throughout the three weeks or so that each Joint Warrior lasts for.

The exercises are ideal for trying out new technology and weaponry, such as aerial or underwater drones, which is why the manufacturers are often invited along to display and get first-hand feedback on their developing products. The Armed Forces of other NATO member countries are also often involved, given that they are ideal opportunities to practise for Joint Task Force operations.

Civilian mariners are kept informed of planned submarine and gunnery activity throughout the exercise by means of broadcasts made by the Belfast, Clyde and Stornoway Coastguard Stations. It's quite important to listen to those if you're thinking of doing a spot of fishing in the middle of a Joint Warrior exercise!

Joint Expeditionary Force (Maritime)

The Navy's Joint Expeditionary Force (JEF), led by the Commander Amphibious Task Group, is the quick-reaction force maintained at a high state of readiness to respond to unexpected global events, from conflict to disaster relief or humanitarian aid. It will typically be deployed as a Joint Operation, i.e. with Army and RAF components as required, or even as a Combined Operation with foreign partners, which is the reason behind the regular multinational exercises that now take place around the world each year. In times of need, elements of these multinational exercises will break away to intervene in the very kinds of global events they are training to deal with, as happened at the time of the Libyan Civil War in 2011 and Typhoon Haiyan in the Philippines in 2013.

The JEF is ideally suited to delivering marines and their equipment ashore by helicopter and landing craft and then directing their operations from the sea. The ability to do so around the world will be greatly enhanced by the arrival of the new Queen Elizabeth-class carriers, which will come equipped with all the logistics and technology necessary for the rapid deployment and ongoing support of aeroplanes, helicopters and landing craft launched from the sea.

NATO

Following the formation of the North Atlantic Treaty Organisation (NATO) in 1949, the Navy started to contribute ships to the Standing Naval Force Atlantic in 1968, and it has been continuously contributing to NATO ever since.

Today it regularly supplies a vessel to Standing NATO Maritime Group 2 (Mediterranean), a multinational Immediate Reaction Force involved in everything from operational training exercises, international relations and peacekeeping to counterterrorism, anti-piracy and crisis response, often in response to UN resolutions.

THE MERCHANT NAVY

Seamen of the Merchant Navy can be called upon to support the Royal Navy at times of conflict, the most notable examples in recent history having been the two world wars and the Falklands Conflict. Almost 15,000 merchant seamen were killed in World War One and around 32,000 in World War Two, mostly on board Atlantic Convoy vessels sunk by U-boats. Their sacrifices are honoured each year when wreaths are laid alongside those of the Armed Services on Remembrance Day, and in their own annual Merchant Navy Day on 3 September. The title of Merchant Navy was bestowed upon them by George V in honour of their service during World War One.

THE SURFACE FLEET

The Surface Fleet is the core of the Navy, comprising its assault ships, destroyers, frigates, patrol vessels, mine countermeasure vessels and survey vessels, which include an ice patrol ship. Of the sixty-four vessels of the Surface Fleet at the time of writing, the major combatants are its three assault ships, six destroyers and thirteen frigates. Together with the Navy's two new aircraft carriers, they will provide the backbone of the fleet for many years to come, committed 365 days a year to the defence of the UK and its overseas territories; to hunt submarines, pirates, smugglers, human traffickers and drug runners; and to provide humanitarian aid in the event of a natural disaster. The Fleet Diving Squadron is also an integral part of the Surface Fleet arm for command purposes, but, as we will see, their remit is as wide as it needs to be.

ASSAULT SHIPS

The three amphibious assault ships of the Navy are the helicopter and amphibious assault ship HMS *Ocean* (nicknamed 'The Mighty O'), which at the time of writing is the flagship of the Navy, and the two amphibious assault ships HMS *Albion* and HMS *Bulwark*. All three are assigned to the Devonport Flotilla.

HMS OCEAN

- ▶ Type: Landing Platform Helicopter
- ▶ Aircraft capacity: 6 attack helicopters, 12 support helicopters
- ▶ Landing craft capacity: 2 hovercraft, 4 personnel landing craft, 40 light vehicles
- ▶ Crew: 285, plus 180 FAA/RAF
- ▶ Troops: 480–800 marines
- ▶ Length: 203 metres
- ▶ Weight: 8,000 tonnes
- ▶ Speed: 16 knots
- ▶ Ships in class:
  - ❖ HMS *Ocean*

HMS *Ocean* has had a varied career, from saving the lives of thirty-four fishermen off the coasts of Honduras and Nicaragua in the aftermath of Hurricane Mitch in 1998 to performing a helicopter assault role during the invasion of Iraq in 2003. She has also been used to train the Somaliland Coastguard and to contribute to the Gallipoli centenary commemorations in Turkey and the Battle of Jutland centenary commemorations at Scapa Flow.

Not content with serving as the flagship of the Navy, *Ocean* has also been the flagship of Combined Task Force 50, a multinational force assigned the role of ensuring security and the flow of trade in the Middle East, a sea area of 2.5 million square miles. It was the first time a Royal Navy warship had taken command of a predominantly US Navy force.

ALBION CLASS

- ► Type: Albion class, Amphibious Transport Dock
- ► Aircraft capacity: 2 helicopters
- ► Landing craft capacity: 8 (for landing personnel, vehicles and tanks)
- ► Crew: 325
- ► Troops: 405 marines
- ► Length: 176 metres
- ► Weight: 19,560 tonnes
- ► Speed: 18 knots
- ► Ships in class:
  - ❖ HMS *Albion*
  - ❖ HMS *Bulwark*

HMS *Albion* and HMS *Bulwark*, which have both enjoyed spells as flagship of the Navy, are amphibious assault ships with one primary purpose in life: to deliver the punch of the marines ashore. As with all Royal Navy ships, though, they have to be a bit more versatile than that.

In recent years, HMS *Bulwark* has been deployed to rescue over 4,000 people from overcrowded boats between Libya and the coastline of southern Europe.

HMS *Albion* has in her time been deployed to evacuate British citizens from the Côte d'Ivoire; bring home stranded members of the Armed Forces and British holidaymakers during the air-travel disruption that followed the 2010 Icelandic volcanic ash incident (as did HMS *Bulwark*); serve as part of the Response Force Task Group off Libya in 2011; and engage in anti-piracy operations off the Horn of Africa that same year.

AIRCRAFT CARRIERS

The Surface Fleet will be augmented in the coming years by two new supercarriers, HMS *Queen Elizabeth* and HMS *Prince of Wales*, the largest ships ever to be built for the Navy. Once operational within the Portsmouth Flotilla, they will plug the recent gap in fixed-wing aircraft carrier operations with F-35B Lightning II stealth fighter jets, while also augmenting the capabilities of seaborne helicopter operations.

As giant floating airfields, they will be a symbol of Britain's continuing naval power and status, enabling sustainable air-strike capability anywhere in the world without the use of other countries' airfields.

QUEEN ELIZABETH CLASS

- ▶ Type: Queen Elizabeth class, Aircraft Carrier
- ▶ Aircraft capacity: 50, to include the following:
  - ❖ F-35B Lightning II stealth fighter jets
  - ❖ Chinook transport helicopters
  - ❖ Apache attack helicopters
  - ❖ Merlin anti-submarine and utility helicopters
  - ❖ Lynx Wildcat attack helicopters
- ▶ Crew: 679 plus aircrew and troops
- ▶ Total personnel capacity: 1,600
- ▶ Length: 280 metres
- ▶ Weight: 65,000 tonnes
- ▶ Speed: 25 knots
- ▶ Ships in class:
  - ❖ HMS *Queen Elizabeth* (due to be operational in 2020)
  - ❖ HMS *Prince of Wales* (due to be operational in 2023)

HMS *QUEEN ELIZABETH*

Here are some more great facts about the biggest ship ever built for the Navy.

▶ She will provide 8 acres of sovereign territory wherever in the world she happens to be.

▶ Along with HMS *Prince of Wales*, she is destined to be the jewel in the crown of the UK's defence capability for fifty years to come, which means her last commanding officer hasn't yet been born.

▶ She is longer than the Houses of Parliament and taller than Niagara Falls (from keel to masthead).

▶ It has taken twenty years to design and build her.

▶ Her leading-edge technology includes an innovative thermal metal coating to make her deck scorch resistant to the heat generated by the powerful thrust of the F-35B Lightning II jets.

▶ Each of the two huge aircraft lifts can take two F-35B jets (or the entire ship's crew) from the hangar to the flight deck in sixty seconds.

▶ The ship's range is 8,000–10,000 nautical miles (about the distance from London to New Zealand).

▶ If the cable used for her on-board systems was laid end to end, it would stretch from London to Gibraltar.

▶ She was assembled at Rosyth Dockyard on the Firth of Forth, with many of the 'blocks' being supplied from other shipbuilding yards around the country.

▶ There are two 'islands' on the deck, one for the ship's bridge and the other for air traffic control.

▶ Her painted surface would cover 208 football pitches.

▶ Each of her two propellers weighs 33 tonnes, which is 2.5 times the weight of a double-decker bus.

▶ The 80,000 tonnes of steel used to build her was three times that required for Wembley Stadium.

▶ Sea trials and operations will be carried out from her home base at HMNB Portsmouth, where she will loom large above everything else in port.

▶ A replica of the carrier's operations room was set up in HMS Collingwood to train the ship's company on the mission system, which includes communications, mission planning, air traffic control, navigation, tactical data and visual surveillance.

DESTROYERS

The primary role of the destroyers, the most advanced warships the nation has ever had, is the protection of the fleet from air attack using the Sea Viper missile, which can knock targets out of the sky 70 miles away. They are also flexible enough to act across a whole range of military activity, from high-intensity battle and artillery bombardment of shore targets to disaster relief and anti-piracy measures. The state-of-the-art Sampson radar system used on the Type 45 is as sophisticated as it gets and is a vital part of the air defence system.

DARING CLASS

- ▶ Type: Daring class, Type 45 Air Defence Destroyer
- ▶ Aircraft capacity: 1 Merlin or 2 Lynx Wildcat helicopters
- ▶ Crew: 190
- ▶ Length: 152 metres
- ▶ Weight: 8,000 tonnes
- ▶ Speed: 30 knots
- ▶ Ships in class:
  - ❖ HMS *Daring*
  - ❖ HMS *Dauntless*
  - ❖ HMS *Diamond*
  - ❖ HMS *Dragon*
  - ❖ HMS *Defender*
  - ❖ HMS *Duncan*

The following operations give a flavour of the range of activities undertaken by these impressive vessels.

- ▶ HMS *Daring* carried out disaster-relief operations in the Philippines after that country was struck by a typhoon in 2013.

- ▶ HMS *Dauntless* and HMS *Daring* provided protection to US aircraft carriers as they struck at terrorist targets in Iraq and Syria.

- ▶ HMS *Diamond* has been engaged in tackling human smuggling and arms trafficking in the southern Mediterranean.

▶ HMS *Defender* has provided air defence to US and French carrier strike groups in the Middle East and has been instrumental in the seizure of over a tonne of hashish in the Indian Ocean.

▶ HMS *Dragon* has engaged in patrols of the Falkland Islands and a multinational training exercise in the Gulf of Guinea, and has helped keep trade flowing through the Strait of Hormuz.

▶ HMS *Duncan* has protected allied and merchant shipping in the Mediterranean, Middle East and Gulf sea areas.

Note: To find out what life on board one of these impressive destroyers is like, see the entry on HMS *Dragon* in the 'Life at Sea' chapter.

FRIGATES

The thirteen Type 23 frigates of the Navy, all named after British dukes, have anti-air, anti-ship and anti-submarine capabilities to protect themselves as well as other frigates, destroyers and carriers. Originally designed to face up to the Soviet submarine threat during the Cold War, these sophisticated ships have been updated to deal with just about any mission imaginable.

DUKE CLASS

▶ Type: Duke class, Type 23 Frigate
▶ Aircraft capacity: 1 Merlin or Lynx Wildcat helicopter
▶ Crew: 185
▶ Length: 133 metres

- ▶ Weight: 4,900 tonnes
- ▶ Speed: 28 knots
- ▶ Ships in class:
- ▶ Portsmouth Flotilla:
  - ❖ HMS *Westminster*
  - ❖ HMS *Richmond*
  - ❖ HMS *Lancaster*
  - ❖ HMS *Kent*
  - ❖ HMS *Iron Duke*
  - ❖ HMS *St Albans*
- ▶ Devonport Flotilla:
  - ❖ HMS *Portland*
  - ❖ HMS *Montrose*
  - ❖ HMS *Sutherland*
  - ❖ HMS *Monmouth*
  - ❖ HMS *Somerset*
  - ❖ HMS *Northumberland*
  - ❖ HMS *Argyll*

Frigate facts

- ▶ HMS *Argyll*, the oldest of the Type 23 frigates, saw action in the Sierra Leone Civil War as long ago as 2000, and in the last few years has been deployed to the Gulf, the Caribbean, the North Atlantic and the South Atlantic. She has been engaged in hurricane disaster relief in Bermuda and a series of drug busts that seized £77 million worth of narcotics.

- In 2015, HMS *Lancaster* was the first Navy vessel to deploy with the new Lynx Wildcat attack helicopter. Her primary sponsor is the Duke of Lancaster, better known as Her Majesty the Queen, who has taken a keen interest in her deployments over the years.

- HMS *Monmouth* has more battle honours than any other current warship, the name having enjoyed seven incarnations since 1666. Reflecting the Duke of Monmouth's rebellion against the crown in 1685, and the subsequent blacking out of his coat of arms, the frigate is also known as 'the Black Duke', flies a black flag in addition to the White Ensign and has black (as opposed to traditional red) nameplates. Her officers also carry black handkerchiefs.

- HMS *Richmond* was on a real high (pun intended) after intercepting £26 million worth of heroin in the Indian Ocean in 2015 and a further £3 million worth of cannabis in the Mediterranean on her way home from there to Portsmouth.

Note: The current thirteen Type 23 frigates will start to be replaced by a combination of Type 26 Global Combat Ships and Type 31 General Purpose Frigates from 2021 onwards.

A LUCKY ESCAPE

Using the recognised classification to distinguish between ships of the same class, HMS *Lancaster* was in line to be allocated the pennant number F232, being the third frigate in the Type 23 class (the first one was F230), until someone remembered that 232 was the Navy report form number for groundings and collisions. With sailors being superstitious about such matters, she was soon renumbered F229.

MINE COUNTERMEASURE VESSELS SQUADRON

The Navy's fifteen Mine Countermeasure Vessels (MCMVs) have glass-reinforced plastic hulls to reduce their magnetic signature while they clear the way for larger vessels of the fleet, which they do by detecting and destroying any nasty surprises that lurk beneath the waterline. One of the MCMVs is always deployed to the NATO Mine Countermeasures Force, usually in northern Europe or the Mediterranean.

The squadron works closely with the Fleet Diving Squadron (more of which later).

SANDOWN CLASS, FASLANE FLOTILLA

- ▶ Type: Sandown class, MCMV
- ▶ Crew: 40
- ▶ Length: 53 metres
- ▶ Weight: 600 tonnes
- ▶ Speed: 13 knots
- ▶ Ships in class:
  - ❖ HMS *Grimsby*
  - ❖ HMS *Blyth*
  - ❖ HMS *Bangor*
  - ❖ HMS *Ramsey*
  - ❖ HMS *Shoreham*
  - ❖ HMS *Pembroke*
  - ❖ HMS *Penzance*

The seven Sandown-class vessels (all named after British coastal towns and cities) are assigned to the 1st Mine Countermeasures Squadron of the Faslane Flotilla. Four of them are deployed to the Northern Gulf to ensure the safe flow of the trade and oil on which the British economy depends (ninety-five per cent of goods and fuel to and from Britain travels by sea). The other three vessels patrol the British coastline and rivers to clear any ordnance that still lingers from the world wars.

HUNT CLASS, PORTSMOUTH FLOTILLA

- ▶ Type: Hunt class, MCMV
- ▶ Crew: 50
- ▶ Length: 60 metres
- ▶ Weight: 750 tonnes
- ▶ Speed: 15 knots
- ▶ Ships in class:
  - ❖ HMS *Chiddingfold*
  - ❖ HMS *Ledbury*
  - ❖ HMS *Brocklesby*
  - ❖ HMS *Quorn*
  - ❖ HMS *Atherstone*
  - ❖ HMS *Cattistock*
  - ❖ HMS *Hurworth*
  - ❖ HMS *Middleton*

The eight Hunt-class MCMVs (named after British fox hunts in line with the original Hunt-class minesweepers built between 1916 and

1919) are assigned to the 2nd Mine Countermeasures Squadron of the Portsmouth Flotilla. They scan the world's seabeds with high-definition sonar to detect mines or other explosives, which are then destroyed by the ships' diving team or by remote-controlled countercharges.

PATROL VESSELS

The twenty-two patrol vessels of the Navy consist of sixteen Archer-class fast inshore patrol craft, four River-class patrol ships and two Scimitar-class fast patrol boats.

ARCHER CLASS

▶ Type: Archer class, P2000 inshore patrol craft
▶ Crew: 12–18
▶ Length: 21 metres
▶ Weight: 54 tonnes
▶ Speed: 25 knots
▶ Ships in class:
  ❖ HMS *Archer*
  ❖ HMS *Biter*
  ❖ HMS *Smiter*
  ❖ HMS *Pursuer*
  ❖ HMS *Blazer*
  ❖ HMS *Dasher*
  ❖ HMS *Puncher*
  ❖ HMS *Charger*

- ❖ HMS *Ranger*
- ❖ HMS *Trumpeter*
- ❖ HMS *Example*
- ❖ HMS *Explorer*
- ❖ HMS *Express*
- ❖ HMS *Exploit*
- ❖ HMS *Tracker*
- ❖ HMS *Raider*

Fourteen of the Archer-class patrol vessels form the First Patrol Boat Squadron of the Portsmouth Flotilla, with a primary role to support the University Royal Naval Units, which provide training in navigation and seamanship to undergraduates at fourteen different university areas around the country. They also support the Surface Fleet in a range of tasks around British and European waters, often showing the flag in places that the larger vessels of the fleet can't reach. In 2016 eight of them conveyed royalty and world leaders across Scapa Flow to take part in the centenary events for the Battle of Jutland.

The other two Archer-class vessels, HMS *Raider* and HMS *Tracker*, form the Faslane Patrol Boat Squadron, part of the team that safeguards Britain's nuclear submarine fleet in Scotland.

THE SWORD OF PEACE

The ships and companies of the First Patrol Boat Squadron were awarded the Sword of Peace for their outstanding performance during 2012. The award is given annually to deserving units of the British Armed Forces for activities beyond their normal role and which improve relationships with British or overseas communities. Four of the ships excelled during a summer deployment to the Baltic, six of them provided security for the London Olympic and Paralympic Games, and two of them provided an Honour Guard for the Thames Diamond Jubilee Pageant.

RIVER CLASS

- ▶ Type: River class, offshore patrol vessel
- ▶ Crew: Up to 42
- ▶ Troops: 20–110
- ▶ Length: 80–102 metres
- ▶ Weight: 1,700–2,000 tonnes
- ▶ Speed: 20–21 knots
- ▶ Ships in class:
  - ❖ HMS *Tyne*
  - ❖ HMS *Severn*
  - ❖ HMS *Mersey*
  - ❖ HMS *Clyde*

All four of the Navy's River-class patrol ships are assigned to the Portsmouth Flotilla. Three of them form the Fishery Protection Squadron, the oldest formation in the Navy, which has responsibility for patrolling up to 200 miles into the Atlantic to enforce maritime security and to ensure that fishing boats and trawlers stick to the quotas and sizing rules that have been agreed internationally to preserve fish stocks for future generations.

The fourth River-class vessel, HMS *Clyde*, is the vessel that patrols the territorial waters and monitors the airspace around the Falkland Islands. She was built later than the other three vessels, with an extended hull to accommodate a Merlin helicopter, two sea boats and up to 110 troops (which accounts for the range of statistics in the list above).

Note: Five more of the larger patrol vessels like HMS *Clyde* are planned to come into service over the next few years.

THE VERSATILITY OF THE FISHERY PROTECTION SQUADRON

The versatility of the three patrol boats of the Fishery Protection Squadron allows them to perform a range of duties beyond their regular job description, as evidenced by the following deployments.

► HMS *Mersey* was deployed to the Standing NATO Maritime Group 2 throughout 2016, visiting thirty-one ports in nineteen countries across three continents.

► HMS *Severn* has been deployed to the Caribbean to provide reassurance to British overseas territories and dependencies in the region.

► HMS *Tyne* is one of the busiest ships in the entire Surface Fleet, operating at sea for over 300 days a year. Twice in 2016 she escorted Russian ships transiting to or from the Mediterranean through the North Sea and English Channel.

SCIMITAR CLASS

- ▶ Type: Scimitar class, fast patrol boat
- ▶ Crew: 7
- ▶ Length: 16 metres
- ▶ Weight: 24 tonnes
- ▶ Speed: 32 knots
- ▶ Ships in class:
  - ❖ HMS *Scimitar*
  - ❖ HMS *Sabre*

HMS *Scimitar* and HMS *Sabre* form the Gibraltar Squadron, protecting the maritime environment and enforcing the sovereignty of British Gibraltar Territorial Waters. They popped home in 2012 to escort the Royal Barge during the Thames Diamond Jubilee Pageant.

SURVEY VESSELS

The Navy has five survey ships, ranging from the Antarctic ice patrol ship *Protector* to the coastal survey ship *Gleaner*, all of which are assigned to the Hydrographic Squadron of the Devonport Flotilla. Hydrography is one of the oldest functions of the Navy, ever since Charles II ordered the first comprehensive survey of the British coastline in 1681, leading to the first 'Admiralty chart' in 1801 and the first sale of the data to merchant marine companies in 1819. Coupled with the latest meteorological information, hydrographic and oceanographic surveys are used today in support of military operations and, as ever, to keep the world's sea lanes safe.

HMS *PROTECTOR*

The Navy's ice patrol ship HMS *Protector* is deployed 330 days a year to meet UK obligations under the Antarctic Treaty System through hydrographic charting, support to scientific research and inspections to ensure that expeditions and vessels meet their environmental obligations. She maintains a sovereign presence in the maritime regions of British Antarctic Territory, South Georgia and the South Sandwich Islands, and she has travelled further south than any other Royal Navy ship in history, having dipped below a latitude of 77 degrees south.

The seabed data collected by the multi-beam echo sounder mounted on her hull (or her survey motor boat) is used by the UK Hydrographic Office in Taunton to update the charts used by the Navy and many other mariners, including the Antarctic cruise ships that deliver tens of thousands of ecotourists to the region each year.

She also carries a ramped landing craft, seven inflatables, a Land Rover and three quad bikes so that the marines deployed to her can have as much operational training as possible in the extreme conditions.

HMS *SCOTT*

In spite of her size (13,500 tonnes over a length of 131 metres), the ocean survey vessel HMS *Scott* requires a crew of only seventy-eight and can remain at sea for 300 days a year by rotating that crew on a regular basis. Using multi-beam sonar, she can scan 150 square kilometres of ocean floor every hour. She is so spacious that each crew member can have his or her own en-suite cabin and stay fit by making use of the two gymnasiums and badminton/basketball court.

HMS *ECHO*

One of two Echo-class hydrographic survey ships, HMS *Echo* carries out a wide range of survey and mine countermeasure work, including support to amphibious and submarine operations, which requires her to be armed for protection. She also carries a detachment of marines when on operations.

Both Echo-class vessels are fitted with azimuth thrusters, an arrangement of propellers housed in pods that can be moved to any horizontal angle, making rudders unnecessary and allowing high manoeuvrability. The survey motor boats they carry can operate independently to support a group of surveyors working ashore for a period of time.

In 2015, while being filmed for a documentary about the Battle of Jutland, *Echo* used her state-of-the-art technology to survey the area off Denmark where the battle took place in 1916 – and found a few surprises, including a remarkably intact HMS *Defence*, which had been reported at the time to be 'reduced to atoms' after her magazines exploded.

HMS *ENTERPRISE*

The other Echo-class hydrographic survey ship, HMS *Enterprise*, is equally versatile, and therefore also armed. In addition to her normal surveying role, she has engaged in NATO exercises, mine countermeasure activity, the evacuation of British citizens from Libya to Malta, and the rescue of over 9,000 migrants trying to cross the Mediterranean from Libya to Italy. In 2016 she was awarded the Sword of Peace for her life-saving work in the Mediterranean.

At the time of writing, HMS *Enterprise* is keeping an eye on the Falkland Islands while the regular patrol vessel HMS *Clyde* enjoys some much-needed maintenance at Simon's Town in South Africa, but she will also update the marine charts of the area while she is there.

HMSML *GLEANER*

The survey motor launch HMSML *Gleaner* has very sophisticated technology, using multi-beam and side-scan sonar to collect data on the nature and depth of the seabed around Britain. As the Navy's smallest ship, being less than 15 metres in length and needing a crew of just nine, she is the only one to bear the prefix HMSML (Her Majesty's Small Motor Launch), but she is a little ship that punches above her weight. Due to be withdrawn from service in 2018 after thirty-five years of service, she has three real claims to fame:

- ▶ Completion of a survey of the shallow seabed around the entire coastline of Britain.

- ▶ She is the only Royal Navy ship to have visited landlocked Switzerland, having travelled up the Rhine to Basle in 1988.

- ▶ She conducted an extensive survey of the Firth of Forth in 2016 to prepare for the departure of the newly built aircraft carrier HMS *Queen Elizabeth* in 2017.

FLEET DIVING SQUADRON

The Fleet Diving Squadron consists of the Northern Diving Group, the Southern Diving Group and the Fleet Diving Group, all of which provide specialist diving support and bomb disposal. Over a hundred world-class divers, proficient in all types of diving and in the operation of recompression chambers, are deployed by the squadron to meet some of the greatest challenges faced by the Navy. In addition to the not inconsiderable task of disposing of unexploded devices at sea, in ports and even on land, these expert divers also undertake underwater ship or submarine maintenance or repairs, and sometimes even submarine rescue operations.

THE NORTHERN DIVING GROUP

This group is based at the Clyde Naval Base at Faslane and covers the coastal area from Liverpool to Hull via Northern Ireland, the Western Isles, the Orkneys and the Shetlands. This huge area suffered a lot of bombing raids during World War Two, and the team is still finding and disposing of that ordnance over seventy years later. The threat of unexploded ordnance is not just to international trade and shipping, but to the general public on dry land, which is why the team has also developed expertise in improvised explosive device disposal in any environment.

The Northern Diving Group also mans the NATO Submarine Rescue System (more of which later) alongside divers of the French and Norwegian Navies. They can be deployed anywhere in the world at short notice to rescue a distressed submarine, which, let's be honest, is a skill not many of us have.

THE SOUTHERN DIVING GROUP

As you may have guessed, this group covers the area clockwise from Hull to Liverpool via the English Channel. It has two units, one based in Plymouth and the other in Portsmouth. They too must deal with World War Two ordnance, including requests to dispose of unexploded devices on dry land.

The Southern Diving Group also has specialists in Maritime Explosive Ordnance Disposal under battle conditions, providing In Water Maintenance And Repair (IWMAR) and Battle Damage Assessment and Repair (BDAR) capabilities. They must be ready to deploy anywhere around the globe at any time to support the Navy's many different types of operational activity.

THE FLEET DIVING GROUP

The Fleet Diving Group, based at Portsmouth, is made up of three elite diving units. Fleet Diving Unit 1 are the maritime counterterrorism specialists. They are parachute-trained and maintain a high state of readiness 365 days a year to deal with terrorist devices anywhere in the world. Fleet Diving Units 2 and 3 provide expertise in harbour and port clearance, including in the searching of berths, jetties and ships, and must also be ready to deploy anywhere at any time.

ALL IN A DAY'S WORK

Bombs away

Here are just three recent examples of the hundreds of pieces of ordnance requiring disposal each year around Britain.

► In October 2015, the Northern Diving Group had to move people from their houses in Gourock on the River Clyde while they towed one of the British mines laid during World War Two out to sea, where it was less likely to affect the house prices in Gourock. They detonated the mine once it was out of harm's way.

► In November 2016, the Southern Diving Group had to detonate a German device found while dredging Portsmouth Harbour in preparation for the arrival of the new aircraft carriers HMS *Queen Elizabeth* and *Prince of Wales*. The device was towed out of the harbour to a point 1.5 miles east of the Isle of Wight, where it was detonated safely. Several devices have been found in the harbour during the work that has been necessary to accommodate the new carriers.

► In January 2017, the Southern Diving Group was called out to dispose of a World War Two bomb dropped into the Thames by a German aircraft. It had just been dredged up off Victoria Embankment near the Houses of Parliament, which meant the team had to remove it from the dredger and tow it out to Tilbury before they could safely detonate it. A sigh of relief doubtless accompanied the realisation that they had not succeeded where Guy Fawkes failed.

THE SUBMARINE SERVICE

We Come Unseen.

THE MOTTO OF THE SUBMARINE SERVICE

The eleven nuclear-powered submarines of today's 'Silent Service', as the Submarine Service is also known, have the stealth, endurance and flexibility to go anywhere at any time. Nuclear propulsion means that these submarines don't have to surface on a regular basis and can operate submerged, even at high speed, over long periods. Their endurance is limited only by the need to stock up the pantry and let the crew have some time off. Four of the eleven submarines are armed with Trident missiles to provide the UK's formidable nuclear deterrent. The entire fleet has been built at Barrow-in-Furness in Cumbria.

By 2022, HMNB Clyde at Faslane in Scotland will be home to all the service's training facilities in addition to its total fleet of eleven submarines and an increased workforce of around 8,500. A major infrastructure development project will also upgrade the port facilities there and replace or refurbish the current nuclear facilities.

BALLISTIC SUBMARINES

> The four Vanguard-class ballistic missile submarines based at Faslane form the UK's strategic nuclear deterrent force.
>
> ▶ HMS *Vanguard*
> ▶ HMS *Vengeance*
> ▶ HMS *Victorious*
> ▶ HMS *Vigilant*

At 150 metres in length, and with a displacement of 15,900 tonnes, these 'bombers' are the largest submarines ever built for the Navy, each one being more than twice the size of a Boeing 747 jumbo jet. They are powered by a Rolls-Royce PWR2 nuclear reactor, which boils seawater to produce enough steam to propel the vessel through the water at up to 25 knots.

Each vessel is equipped with four Spearfish heavy torpedo tubes for anti-submarine and anti-surface-ship warfare, and sixteen Trident II ballistic missile tubes, each missile being armed with up to eight thermonuclear warheads. The Trident missiles can travel at over 13,000 miles per hour and their warheads can hit eight separate targets up to 7,000 miles away. Each warhead has an explosive power several times that of the atomic bombs dropped on Japan in 1945.

Only the prime minister can authorise the launch of a nuclear weapon. In the event of a devastating attack in which the Palaces of Westminster are destroyed and the prime minister and their second in command are killed, each submarine will instead carry out the orders contained in a 'letter of last resort' written by each incoming prime minister. The patrols of a Vanguard-class submarine are so secretive that only four out of 135 of the boat's company know what route the submarine will take on voyages that can last for months.

Note: Even larger Dreadnought-class ballistic submarines will start to replace the Vanguard class around 2030 and the first in class will be called HMS *Dreadnought*.

FLEET SUBMARINES

The seven nuclear-powered fleet submarines are known as 'attack submarines' or 'hunter-killer submarines', because they can be used to attack and sink surface vessels as well as other submarines. They can operate independently or as part of a battle fleet.

There are currently four Trafalgar-class and three Astute-class fleet submarines, but by 2024 all four Trafalgar-class boats are due to have been replaced by the more modern Astute class.

TRAFALGAR CLASS

► HMS *Talent*
► HMS *Torbay*
► HMS *Trenchant*
► HMS *Triumph*

The Trafalgar-class submarines were designed for the Cold War, with sonar so sensitive they can hear vessels 50 miles away. They are armed with Spearfish torpedoes and Tomahawk cruise missiles.

Weighing almost 2 tonnes, each Spearfish torpedo can be fired a distance of 30 miles to deliver an explosive charge that will blast a ship or submarine out of the water.

The Tomahawk Land Attack Cruise Missile (TLAM) can be launched from the sea at land targets over 1,000 miles away with pinpoint accuracy. While in flight, it can beam back images of a target or battlefield and be redirected if necessary.

HMS *Triumph* was one of the attack submarines that launched Tomahawk missiles at al-Qaeda and Taliban targets in Afghanistan in 2001, and again at targets in Libya in 2003.

Note: The Trafalgar-class boats at the time of writing are based at HMNB Devonport, from where they will either see out their service (HMS *Torbay* and *Trenchant*) or transfer to HMNB Clyde (HMS *Talent* and *Triumph*).

ASTUTE CLASS

- ▶ HMS *Astute*
- ▶ HMS *Ambush*
- ▶ HMS *Artful*

At 97 metres long and with a displacement of 7,400 tonnes and a top speed of 30 knots, the Astute-class submarines based at Faslane are the largest, most advanced and most powerful attack submarines ever operated by the Navy. They too are armed with Spearfish torpedoes and Tomahawk cruise missiles.

THE DECOMMISSIONING OF NUCLEAR SUBMARINES

Nuclear-powered submarines can only be dismantled once their radioactive material and components have been safely removed, and there are currently nineteen decommissioned submarines awaiting disposal at Devonport and Rosyth. There are plans to store their

Reactor Pressure Vessels (the thick steel containers that held the nuclear fuels necessary to power the reactors) on an interim basis at an existing radioactive material management site in Cheshire until their permanent disposal in a UK Geological Disposal Facility sometime after 2040. Geological Disposal Facilities will be built by many countries in the decades ahead to dispose of nuclear waste deep inside a suitable rock environment to ensure that no harmful quantities of radioactivity can ever reach the surface.

THE (NATO) SUBMARINE RESCUE SYSTEM

The Submarine Rescue System has been developed jointly by the UK, Norway and France but is also available to NATO and allied nations' submarines with a suitable 'mating' surface around their hatch. Based at HMNB Clyde, the 10-metre-long, 30-tonne vessel can be delivered by air and then sea to the location of a distressed submarine within three to four days. Trapped submariners can then be evacuated through their submarine's hatch and brought to the surface twelve at a time in the Submarine Rescue Vehicle.

NAVY SPEAK
SUBMARINE LANGUAGE

Submariners have their own version of Navy speak to refer specifically to life underwater, like firing 'fish' (torpedoes) from the 'bomb shop' (the torpedo storage compartment on a submarine). They refer to the sailors of the Surface Fleet 'upstairs' (or 'on the roof') as 'targets' or 'skimmers', which is how they get their own back for the skimmers referring to submariners as 'boat people', because, as any skimmer will tell you, only 'ships' can 'sail' on the surface.

THE SUBMARINE SCHOOL

The Submarine School at HMS Raleigh in Torpoint provides instruction to officers and ratings in pretty much everything, including basic training and core values, radar, electronic and acoustic sensing, weapons engineering, and warfare and submarine command.

Those who pass the training and qualifying boards at Torpoint receive the coveted 'dolphin' badge of the Submarine Service.

The Submarine Command Course

Established in 1917 because high attrition rates during World War One meant that not enough submarine commanders were surviving to pass on their knowledge, the Submarine Command Course was, and still is, one of the toughest command courses anywhere. If you're going to let someone take control of the most complex military hardware your country possesses, it's only right to put them through their paces first.

The course is known as 'the Perisher', because of its relatively high failure rate (thirty per cent) and because failure prevents RN candidates from ever serving again at sea on submarines, although they can instead transfer to the Surface Fleet. Because the course sets such high standards, including sea time under simulated war conditions off Norway and Scotland, many other navies around the world send their potential commanders to Torpoint to have their mettle tested. The course is run twice a year for just six candidates at a time.

Note: The Submarine School is due to be transferred by 2022 to the planned single hub at Faslane.

ALL IN A DAY'S WORK

Commander Norman Douglas Holbrook (1888–1976)

Fourteen submariners have been awarded the Victoria Cross. The first was Norman Holbrook, who commanded his ageing submarine in a treacherous current under five rows of moored mines to torpedo and sink an enemy ship in the Dardanelles in 1914. Under attack from gunfire and torpedo boats much of the way back to the Mediterranean, Holbrook and his men ended up being submerged for nine hours in the small, obsolete submarine by the time it was safe to come up, although they had surfaced briefly from time to time to get their bearings because their compass was broken.

His fame soon spread, and in 1915 the town of Holbrook in New South Wales, Australia, was renamed in his honour (it had been called Germanton, which the residents weren't very happy about during World War One). Holbrook Road in Portsmouth is also named after him, and a stone memorial to commemorate his action has been erected in Southsea, where he was born.

Five of his brothers were also decorated during World War One, earning them the collective nickname of 'the fighting Holbrooks'.

THE JOLLY ROGER

In the early days of submarine warfare, the Admiral of the Fleet Sir Arthur Wilson accused submariners of being 'underhand, unfair and damned un-English' and suggested that they should be treated as pirates by their own countries.

Since then, starting with HMS *E9* on its return to port in 1914 after sinking a German cruiser, many Navy submarines that saw direct action flew their own Jolly Roger to cock a snook at the admiral. The flags were traditionally furnished with daggers for each 'cloak and dagger' operation and torpedoes or simple bars for each sinking of an enemy vessel, with many other variations on the theme.

In 1982, in spite of being ordered not to, HMS *Conqueror* returned from the Falklands flying a Jolly Roger, furnished with one dagger for her deployment of an SBS force to South Georgia and one torpedo for the sinking of the *General Belgrano*. In 1991, HMS *Opossum* and *Otus* returned from the Gulf flying Jolly Rogers, the only indication that they had probably been involved in SBS and SAS operations.

Although, strictly speaking, the practice of flying the Jolly Roger was always prohibited, that prohibition is now enforced to safeguard the secrecy of submarine operations.

THE OFFICIAL TARTAN OF THE SUBMARINE SERVICE

In recognition of more than a century of links between the Submarine Service and Scotland, and of Faslane becoming the UK's single integrated submarine operating base, the Submarine Service launched its own official tartan in 2017.

THE ROYAL MARINES

Per mare, per terram.
(By sea, by land.)

The Royal Marines are one of the world's elite commando forces, ready to respond to situations anywhere around the globe with five days' notice. Specialists in amphibious, cold-weather and mountain warfare, they have taken part in more battles around the world than any other branch of the British Armed Forces.

Although its history is inextricably linked with that of the Royal Navy, it is also unique in many ways, which is why we are going to look at it now in the round before going on to consider the multifaceted role that the Marines play today.

THE HISTORY OF THE ROYAL MARINES

1664:   The origin of the corps lies in the 1664 Order in Council to raise 1,200 men for the Lord Admiral's

Regiment of Sea Soldiers, to be known as the Duke of York and Albany's Maritime Regiment of Foot.

1755: The corps was made permanent and reorganised to serve on warships. Their main tasks now were to maintain discipline and provide sentries on board and play in the ship's band.

1802: George III honoured the corps with the title and status of Royal Marines.

1804: The first Marine Artillery Companies were formed to operate mortars that were mounted near the bow of sailing warships to launch explosive shells at land targets. This tradition of marines manning guns on warships continued as technology evolved, with at least one gun turret on most warships manned by marines during the world wars of the twentieth century and all the way through to the 1970s.

1890s: The uniform was changed from red-and-blue tunics to grey and then khaki as red and blue had been making the marines easy targets for increasingly skilful sharpshooters. (At the time of the 300th anniversary of the corps in 1964, the uniform changed colour again to its current lovat green, although officers continue to wear blue on ceremonial occasions.)

1914–18: World War One saw the beginnings of the Marines' transition to their now traditional role of amphibious assault. We have already seen in Part One the crucial role they played in the Royal Naval Division's efforts at Antwerp, Gallipoli, Zeebrugge and the Western Front.

1939–45:   As we also saw in Part One, World War Two brought the formation of the first RM Commando units (within the Combined Services Commando Brigades) to raid enemy coastal positions and establish beachheads. They have as their legacy today the remaining RM Commando units and Special Boat Service, in addition to the Parachute Regiment and Special Air Service of the British Army.

CORPS MEMORABLE DATES

The proud history of the Marines is reflected in their official Memorable Dates, which must be learned by heart by all new recruits.

Memorable Date	Action	Description
28 October 1664	The birth of the corps	Established by King Charles II.
24 July 1704	The capture of Gibraltar	The date on which the Marines took Gibraltar from the Spanish and the beginning of the heavy eight-month siege they had to endure thereafter. The battle honour remains to this day on the Marines' cap badge and colours.
7 June 1761	The Battle of Belle Isle	The laurel wreath displayed on the colours and badges of the corps commemorate the spirit and gallantry shown by the two RM battalions that fought during the siege, assault and capture of Belle Isle near Quiberon Bay in Brittany (during the Seven Years' War against France).

Memorable Date	Action	Description
17 June 1775	The Battle of Bunker Hill	The marines of the 1st and 2nd Battalions displayed great courage in driving the Americans from this high ground north of Boston during the American Revolutionary War.
21 October 1805	The Battle of Trafalgar	Nearly 3,000 marines fought at Trafalgar, boarding and capturing French ships, defending the decks of British ships against French boardings and shooting at French snipers high in their riggings. In fact, the Marines fought in all of Nelson's sea battles.
28 April 1915	The Battle of Gallipoli	The start of two weeks of heavy fighting at Gallipoli for the RM Light Infantry Units of the Royal Naval Division. Lance Corporal William Parker, a stretcher-bearer, was awarded the VC for tending and evacuating the wounded from a trench under fire, being wounded himself in the process.
23 April 1918	The assault on Zeebrugge	A recognition of tremendous gallantry under heavy fire when 4th Battalion attacked the German naval base at Zeebrugge. Two Victoria Crosses were awarded, but there were so many acts of bravery that day that the recipients had to be decided by votes cast by the surviving marines.

Memorable Date	Action	Description
13 December 1939	The Battle of the River Plate	Marines served on board all three of the British cruisers that took hits from the *Admiral Graf Spee*. Sticking to their task under heavy bombardment helped the Navy to disable the German battleship in the end.
6 June 1944	The Normandy Landings	Marines were amongst the first troops on to the beaches on D-Day and crewed two-thirds of all landing craft.
1 November 1944	The assault on Walcheren	In the decisive Battle of the Scheldt, this amphibious commando action finally silenced German coastal batteries at the mouth of the river, but losses were heavy as many landing craft were sunk or crippled by artillery fire before the marines could reach land.
14 June 1982	The recapture of the Falkland Islands	Marines established the bridgehead at San Carlos and played a crucial role in defeating the Argentinian ground forces on East Stanley and South Georgia (see below for individual unit battle honours).

UNIT BATTLE HONOURS IN THE FALKLANDS CONFLICT

▶ 3 Commando Brigade HQ: Landing in San Carlos Water: 21 May 1982

▶ Signals Squadron RM: Landing in San Carlos Water: 21 May 1982

▶ Operational Landing Craft Squadrons: Landing in San Carlos Water: 21 May 1982

▶ Commando Logistics Regiment RM: Landing at Ajax Bay: 22 May 1982

▶ 42 Commando RM: Attack on Mount Harriet: 11 and 12 June 1982

▶ 45 Commando RM: Attack on Two Sisters: 11 and 12 June 1982

▶ 3 Commando Brigade Air Squadron RM: Recapture of the Falkland Islands: 14 June 1982

GETTING THE DIFFICULT JOBS DONE

The Marines have seen action in almost every corner of the world, a fact recognised by the globe and laurel displayed on the colours and cap badges of the corps. They also have a long history of carrying out operations at the more difficult end of the scale, as you might expect of an elite force.

▶ Press-ganging men into service and restoring order following mutinies within the Navy.

▶ Sailing captured ships home to Britain and holding captured forts and islands until relieved by more permanent troops during the Napoleonic era.

▶ Setting up the first penal colony at Botany Bay in Australia in the late eighteenth century (the Marines can be counted amongst the founding fathers of colonial Australia as many either took their wives along or ended up marrying the female convicts).

▶ Providing artillery at the famous battles of Inkerman and Balaclava during the Crimean War, and winning three of the newly instituted Victoria Crosses during that campaign. The first was won by Corporal John Prettyjohn at the Battle of Inkerman – having run out of ammunition after personally shooting four Russians, he had his men beat the Russians back down a hill by showering them with rocks, except for the one Russian he threw down with his bare hands.

▶ 'Imperial policing' in the Ashanti, Zulu and Boer Wars in Africa, the First Opium War and the Boxer Rebellion in China, and the Indian Mutiny.

▶ Manning guns on board battleships at the Battle of Jutland in 1916 (in one particularly heroic action, Major Francis Harvey was posthumously awarded the VC for ordering the flooding of the magazines to prevent HMS *Lion* from blowing up while he himself was mortally wounded).

▶ Fighting in the difficult jungle environments of Burma, Malaya and Borneo.

▶ Establishing their reputation as a modern rapid-response task force, with swift and effective actions in conflict zones that have included Suez, Aden, the Gulf, East Africa, the Falklands, Afghanistan and Iraq.

⚓ FAMOUS SAILORS ⚓

GENERAL SIR
EDWARD NICOLLS
(1779–1865)

No one typified the spirit of the Royal Marines more than 'Fighting Nicolls' during his forty years of service across the world between 1795 and 1835. He was in action 107 times and wounded twenty-four times, including a broken left leg, being shot through the body and right arm, suffering a severe sabre cut to the head, being bayoneted in the chest and losing the sight of an eye. Having joined up at the age of just fifteen, he saw action throughout the Napoleonic Wars and fought in battles as far apart as the Dardanelles and the Caribbean. He was promoted to full general on his retirement in 1855.

UNSUNG HEROES

Not least because Royal Marines wear the combat dress of a soldier, their presence often goes largely unnoticed by the public and even the media. The same is true for the entire Naval Service when serving in countries like Iraq and Afghanistan, because members of the Armed Forces all wear the same desert camouflage that is mostly associated with the Army. It is a little-known fact, for example, that over fifty per cent of the British Armed Forces in Afghanistan over the winter of 2005–06 were Naval Service, including RM Commandos, Fleet Air Arm aircrew and engineers, mine clearance divers, medical and logistics officers, and HQ staff.

THE ROYAL MARINES TODAY

The organisation of the Marines today has the following component parts, which we will look at one by one in greater detail below.

- ▶ 3 Commando Brigade

- ▶ 539 Assault Squadron

- ▶ 30 Commando IX Group

- ▶ 29 Commando Regiment Royal Artillery

- ▶ 24 Commando Engineer Regiment

- ▶ Commando Logistic Regiment

- ▶ Special Boat Service

- ▶ 1 Assault Group

- ▶ Royal Marines Band Service

3 COMMANDO BRIGADE

Able to deliver punch wherever and whenever it is needed around the globe, 3 Commando Brigade currently has three elite battalion-sized units (40, 42 and 45 Commando) supported by a number of specialist units that could keep them fighting almost indefinitely if the need arose. Trained for amphibious, mountain and cold-weather operations, one of the three commando units is always assigned to the UK's Joint Rapid Reaction Force, ready to be deployed anywhere in the world at short notice.

40 Commando is based at RM Norton Manor near Taunton; 42 Commando is based at Bickleigh Barracks near Plymouth; and 45 Commando is based at RM Condor, Arbroath. 3 Commando

Brigade HQ is based at RM Stonehouse in Plymouth, as is 30 Commando IX Group (see below).

The brigade also has under its command 43 Commando Fleet Protection Group, so called because its primary function is to protect the UK's strategic nuclear deterrent base at the Clyde Naval Base in Scotland, although they also deploy around the world as maritime boarding, cold-weather warfare and sniper teams.

Note: The RM bases at Stonehouse and Norton Manor are due to be closed down in 2023 and 2028 respectively, as part of the Better Defence Estate project, whereupon those based there will likely move to either HMNB Devonport or HMS Raleigh in Cornwall.

COMMANDO KIT AND WEAPONS

Each RM Commando carries an SA-80 assault rifle (with or without an under-slung grenade launcher), a 9-mm pistol and 240 rounds of ammunition. They wear a Kevlar helmet for protection and their bergen (a military rucksack weighing up to 80 pounds/36 kilograms) contains the equipment needed to survive and fight in pretty much any environment, on sea or land, above or below the treeline. They also carry a 'green slug' (sleeping bag), a bivvy bag and enough food for two days.

The marines operate in four-man teams, with each team carrying a four-man tent, naphtha fuel for cooking and lighting, and fluorescent panels for marking out helicopter landing sites. Each commando unit also has mortars, light anti-tank weapons (which are also effective against hovering helicopters), machine guns and sniper rifles.

The mountain and arctic warfare specialists also carry snow shovels and insulated snowshoes that can be attached to their boots. These teams will have learned how to survive in snow holes that they have dug for themselves.

GOING COMMANDO

Not to be outdone by the launch of the Submarine Service's tartan in 2017, 43 Commando unveiled their own official tartan at Faslane in the same year. It is not a first for the Royal Marines, though, who already have the Bootneck 350 Tartan, launched in 2014 as the Marines celebrated 350 years of history, and the Royal Marines Condor Tartan of 45 Commando based in Arbroath. It is widely assumed that the commandos will adhere to the age-old Scottish tradition of going commando under their kilts, as anything less would amount to barefaced cheek.

539 ASSAULT SQUADRON

539 Assault Squadron has the job of transferring the marines of 3 Commando Brigade on to land from sea or river positions, using a range of landing craft from the Navy's amphibious shipping (currently HMS *Ocean*, *Albion* and *Bulwark*) or the Bay-class ships of the Royal Fleet Auxiliary.

30 COMMANDO IX GROUP

30 Commando Information Exploitation Group has the role of providing the intelligence required to enable 3 Commando Brigade operations. It achieves this through the capabilities of its four specialist squadrons.

▶ Surveillance and Reconnaissance Squadron: Operates ahead of the main task force.

▶ Y Squadron: Intercepts enemy communications systems and runs HQ where deployed.

▶ Communications Squadron: Provides communications systems in the field.

▶ Logistics Squadron: Moves, protects and sustains commandos in the field, making use of amphibious, armoured, all-terrain vehicles.

29 COMMANDO REGIMENT ROYAL ARTILLERY

The gunners of 29 Commando Regiment Royal Artillery provide offensive fire support to 3 Commando Brigade with 105-mm light machine guns. They also coordinate fire support from mortars, fast jets, attack helicopters and guns on board ships. There are five Commando Gunner Batteries: 8, 23 and 79 Batteries are based in Plymouth; 148 Battery in Poole; and 7 Battery in Arbroath.

24 COMMANDO ENGINEER REGIMENT

Tasked with ensuring that 3 Commando Brigade can 'fire, fight and move', 24 Commando Engineer Regiment delivers just about any form of construction or demolition in any environment. Its operations include route maintenance, bridging, provision of water and electricity supplies, field defences and mine clearance. It even has divers capable of sub-surface engineering tasks.

COMMANDO LOGISTIC REGIMENT

Based at Chivenor in North Devon, the Commando Logistic Regiment has the role of providing equipment and medical and logistical support to 3 Commando Brigade in the field. As the UK's sole amphibious logistic unit, the regiment has proved its worth on sea and land in the Falklands, Iraq and Afghanistan.

Note: The marines of 3 Commando Brigade will often operate alongside the British Army and be reinforced as necessary by battle tanks, all-terrain vehicles, support or armed helicopters and the infantry of the Rifles Regiment.

SPECIAL BOAT SERVICE

By strength and guile.
THE MOTTO OF THE SBS

Created during World War Two, the Special Boat Service (SBS) exists to carry out secret reconnaissance missions and daring undercover operations using the element of surprise made possible with small, highly trained teams. The Royal Marines provide the bulk of their manpower. The SBS is the Naval Service's equivalent of the Army's Special Air Service (SAS), and only those who display physical and mental aptitudes at the highest levels need apply. Around 200–250 personnel make up the four squadrons of the SBS (C, M, X and Z) at any one time, each one of them expert in boat operation, underwater swimming, diving, parachuting, navigation, demolition and reconnaissance.

Little is known about many of their operations for obvious reasons, at least not until some time after the event, although one high-profile operation did make the headlines during the Gulf War, when the SBS liberated the British embassy in Kuwait after abseiling from the helicopters that had flown them there. Often operating behind enemy lines at great personal risk, it is not difficult to grasp their worth in the ongoing global struggle against terrorism.

1 ASSAULT GROUP

1 Assault Group is tasked with providing training and development in amphibious warfare and surface assault operations. Specific training includes the following.

- ▶ Landing craft, small boats, engineering and assault navigation: Provided by 10 (Landing Craft) Training Squadron at RM Tamar in Devonport.

- ▶ From craft to beachhead training: Delivered by 11 Amphibious Trials and Training Squadron in Instow, North Devon, who also conduct trials of new landing craft.

- ▶ Board and search operations: Provided by the Royal Navy School of Board and Search at HMS Raleigh in Torpoint, Devon.

ROYAL MARINES BAND SERVICE

With its origins dating back to the sixteenth century, when drummers signalled watch changes and beat the men to quarters as the Spanish Armada approached, the Royal Marines Band Service today is the world's most versatile military music organisation, providing first-class music in conjunction with crucial duties during active service.

As the public face of the Naval Service, its marching bands perform a key role in Britain's defence diplomacy, regularly playing before heads of state, royalty and foreign dignitaries. Buglers and musicians alike perform at very high standards after spending two to three years at the Royal Marines School of Music at Portsmouth, and annual performances include the Royal British Legion Festival of Remembrance and the Edinburgh Military Tattoo. Other high-profile jobs have included playing during the long sail into action at the Battle of Trafalgar in 1805 and playing out the final credits of the 1966 film *Thunderbirds Are Go!*

There are currently six bands, based as follows.

- ► RM School of Music, Portsmouth

- ► HMS Nelson, Portsmouth (Barracks)

- ► HMS Raleigh, Torpoint (Training Centre)

- ► HMS Caledonia, Rosyth (Dockyard)

- ► HMS Collingwood, Fareham (Maritime Warfare School)

- ► Commando Training Centre, Lympstone

When not playing in one of the bands, members of the service provide vital operational, medical or logistical support. They lost 225 personnel, a quarter of their total strength, in action during World War Two, and they provided medical aid on board casualty receiving ships during the Falklands Conflict. Other operational deployments have included Cyprus, Kosovo, the Gulf, Afghanistan and the manning of Green Goddess trucks (mobile pumping stations with firefighting capability) during the firemen's strike of 2002–03.

A low point came when the IRA bombed the Royal Marines School of Music at Deal Barracks in 1989, killing eleven and injuring twenty-two Band Service members.

COMMANDO TRAINING CENTRE

RM Commandos are trained at the Commando Training Centre at Lympstone in Devon. Those wishing to wear the coveted Marines green beret, or 'green lid', must complete thirty-two weeks of gruelling training, almost double that required of regular infantry troops in the Army, and overcome the world-famous commando course there, including the following obstacles.

- ▶ Peter's Pool: A partially dammed stream that must be forded chest-high while keeping a rifle high and dry.

- ▶ Smartie Tube: A long, filthy concrete pipe containing mud, stones and running water. It has to be negotiated on their back with their rifle barrel kept dry throughout, or else they go through again.

- ▶ Heartbreak Lane: The final leg of the course, when wet and muddy recruits can suddenly see only hedges on either side after running downhill for 4 miles with the camp buildings in sight. The road also now feels as if it is climbing as well as heading away from the camp. By way of encouragement, though, there is a sign which states: 'It's only pain!'

The commando course is not the only challenge that the recruits face, though, and there are three tests in particular that are renowned for breaking those who don't make it through to the end.

- ▶ The 9-miler: Involves a speed-march in boots and fighting order (meaning with rifles, ammunition, magazines, water bottle, field dressing, poncho cape and mess tins), with the 9-mile road distance having to be completed in under 90 minutes.

- ▶ The Tarzan Assault Course: A test of agility and coordination against the clock, including the aerial ropeway known as Postman's Walk.

- ▶ The 30-miler: The final pass-out test. It is a 30-mile group yomp across Dartmoor in fighting order and carrying safety stores and a radio. It must be completed within 8 hours.

YOs

Young Officers (YOs) train alongside the other recruits at Lympstone, but their training is far longer and they must complete all the commando tests to a higher standard. The 9-miler, for example, must be achieved within 81 minutes, as opposed to the 'generous' 90 minutes afforded to the non-officer recruits, and the 30-miler must be completed within 7.5 hours instead of 8. Each set of YOs is collectively known as 'the Batch', with their trainers referring to them as 'Young Sirs'. The members of each Batch will identify themselves by their Batch number for the rest of their lives and usually have a reunion at the training centre twenty-five years after successful completion of the course.

THE FLEET AIR ARM (FAA)

Today, from their two bases at Yeovilton in Somerset and Culdrose in Cornwall, the FAA deploys an ultra-modern fleet of helicopters to the decks of Navy ships worldwide. Flying from those ships, they carry out a wide range of roles, from the landing of marines on hostile shores to humanitarian aid. The FAA also flies Hawk jets to provide air-attack and threat-simulation training for Navy ships at sea, and going forward they will fly F-35 Joint Strike Fighters from the decks of the new Queen Elizabeth-class carriers.

RNAS CULDROSE

RNAS Culdrose has been the site of a Royal Naval Air Station since 1947 and is now the biggest helicopter base in Europe. Its elevated position on the Lizard peninsula often leads to peculiar weather conditions, such as fog that travels at up to 40 miles per hour, and therefore affords some 'interesting' flying opportunities.

Officially known as HMS Seahawk, Culdrose is effectively the biggest 'ship' in the Navy. It is home to the Merlin HM Mk2 and Sea King Helicopter Forces as well as the FAA's Fixed Wing Force. With over 3,000 men and women on site, it is the biggest single-site employer in Cornwall, injecting around £100 million into the local economy each year. There is also a satellite airfield nearby at RNAS Predannack, which is used as an additional landing ground for training purposes and for firefighting training on retired and dummy aircraft.

The Merlins and Sea Kings based at Culdrose fulfil the roles of Anti-Surface Warfare, Anti-Submarine Warfare, and Airborne Surveillance and Control around the world, in addition to responding to all manner of crises on an ad hoc basis, from humanitarian relief to counternarcotics operations.

THE LONG-REIGNING SEA KINGS
The Sea King helicopters of 849 Naval Air Squadron (NAS) are the last to be operated for military purposes in the UK and are due to be replaced by Merlins in the coming years. They are long-serving, all-weather, versatile, twin-engined helicopters that have served the FAA well since 1966. The four different versions produced have been custom-built for either anti-submarine warfare (ASW), troop transport, airborne early warning (AEW) or search and rescue (SAR). Those of 849 NAS are fitted with AEW Radar, earning them the accolade of being the Navy's 'eyes in the sky'. The fact that the AEW Radar system looks like a huge black bag when it is inflated in mid-air has earned the helicopters and their crews the nickname of 'Baggers'.

MERLIN HM MK2 SUBMARINE HUNTERS
The AgustaWestland Merlin HM Mk2 helicopter is primarily a submarine hunter deployed to the Navy's ships at sea, but it's versatile enough to carry out counterterrorism, search and rescue, anti-piracy, counternarcotics, surveillance, transportation and evacuation duties – it can carry sixteen armed troops or twelve on stretchers.

With a fully digital cockpit and sophisticated radar and sonar capabilities that allow it to find and track potential targets on and below the surface of the sea, it is armed with torpedoes, depth charges and machine guns.

The Merlin HM Mk2 is flown by three front-line squadrons out of Culdrose.

▶ The Flying Tigers (814 NAS): Globally deployed to provide protection from surface and sub-surface threats and to support maritime security operations.

▶ The Flying Fish (820 NAS): Recent deployments have included anti-piracy operations off Somalia, humanitarian aid in the fight against Ebola in Sierra Leone and maritime surveillance in the Middle East. Going forward, the squadron will provide protection to the new supercarriers.

▶ The Kingfishers (829 NAS): Provide the Navy's Type 23 frigates with the Merlins they need to fulfil their obligations across the globe.

Note: The Merlin HM Mk2 is being upgraded with a long-range airborne surveillance system known as Crowsnest. This air, maritime and land capability to detect and track potential targets will allow them to continue as the eyes and ears of the Navy for many years to come, which is one of the reasons that the Merlin Mk2 will be deployed to the two new supercarriers.

In addition to the front-line helicopter squadrons, there are also several very important specialist units based at Culdrose.

MERLIN HELICOPTER TRAINING (824 NAS)

The trainers of 824 NAS feed the front-line Merlin squadrons with the men and women needed to fly and maintain the Merlin HM Mk2. Those who succeed in gaining their coveted 'wings' at the end of a tough forty-four-week course are sent to the front-line squadrons for operational duties.

THE HAWKS (736 NAS)

Although its official title is the Maritime Aggressor Squadron, 736 NAS is in fact a training unit. Equipped with fourteen Hawk fast jets, like the ones used by the RAF's Red Arrows, they simulate airborne threats for the Navy's ships as they prepare for operations or as part of Joint Warrior exercises. The jets are also deployed to assist in the training of ship-based fighter controllers and helicopter-borne AEW observers.

OBSERVER TRAINING (750 NAS)

Observers in the Navy do far more than 'observe', which is why 750 NAS trains them in the vital arts of communication, navigation and tactics, including in-the-air training in King Air Avenger aircraft. Only then can they hope one day to single-handedly operate airborne combat systems. Successful candidates from the observer course at Culdrose can go on to specialise in anti-submarine warfare or fighter control, which may also involve the need to operate airborne machine guns.

UNMANNED AIRCRAFT (700X NAS)

The FAA's first foray into remote piloted air systems, or 'drones', was carried out by 700X ('X' for 'Xperimental') NAS. Starting in 2014, ScanEagle aircraft were catapulted from ships to send back high-quality live video to their ship's operations room by day or night. Able to operate for up to 12 hours at a range of 40 miles from the mother ship, they were first deployed to provide eyes in the sky for the Navy's Mine Countermeasures Vessels in the Gulf, but they were also found to be of use in anti-piracy and counternarcotics operations.

> The X-men of 700X NAS at Culdrose also tested and evaluated new versions of unmanned aircraft to keep the Navy aware of developing technology in this important area, and the Navy has stated a desire for the capability to continue.

BREAKDOWN SERVICES (1710 NAS)

The Maritime Aviation Support Force (1710 NAS) is the breakdown recovery service of the FAA, ready to deploy anywhere in the world at short notice to carry out running repairs on faulty aircraft.

They also have a forensics team, which examines issues such as why an oil leak or crack might suddenly have appeared on an aircraft, whether military or commercial.

In addition to their repair and forensics work, the squadron also provides a service modifications capability to enhance and improve helicopters by adding new equipment or systems. This includes meeting urgent operational requirements or mitigating risk to life, such as when an additional gun or sensor system might be required quickly on a helicopter, whether at sea or on land. However quickly they need to work, though, they must always meet the rigorous safety requirements for aircraft. Their work rarely stops.

NAVY SPEAK
JESUS NUT

One of the things that the helicopter crews of the FAA want the Maritime Aviation Support team to pay particular attention to is the 'Jesus nut', the main retaining nut that secures the rotor to many types of helicopter. It takes its name from the fact that failure of the component will result in the crew meeting the man concerned.

KEEPING STANDARDS UP

Naval Flying Standards Flight (Rotary Wing) conducts annual assessments of all FAA helicopter crew to ensure that the pilots, observers and other aircrew continue to meet the stringent standards demanded of them. Naval Flying Standards Flight (Fixed Wing) performs the same role for the Navy's fixed-wing aircrew at Yeovilton.

CARRYING THE TORCH FOR BRITAIN

In 2012, the airbase at Culdrose made the headlines when the Olympic Flame arrived from Athens on a British Airways Airbus along with Princess Anne, Sebastian Coe and David Beckham. The flame was then carried from there on the first leg of its marathon journey around the UK.

RNAS YEOVILTON

HMS Heron, the Royal Naval Air Station at Yeovilton, is one of the busiest military airfields in the country and is home base to more than a hundred aircraft operated by front-line squadrons and training units, including the squadrons of the Commando Helicopter Force and the Lynx Wildcat Maritime Force. Yeovilton is also home to the Fleet Air Arm Museum and the vintage aircraft of the Royal Navy Historic Flight. There is a satellite airfield, RNAS Merryfield, nearby at Ilton, which is used as a training facility for helicopter pilots.

LYNX WILDCAT MARITIME FORCE

The AgustaWestland Lynx Wildcat Maritime Attack Helicopter is deployed to the Navy's amphibious ships, destroyers and frigates and will also operate from the Navy's two new supercarriers for many years to come. It is an all-weather, two-crew, twin-engined aircraft capable of high speeds, great agility and the despatch of missiles, depth charges and torpedoes. With cutting-edge targeting systems and 360-degree radar, the Wildcat can be used in a wide variety of operations, including anti-ship, anti-submarine, ship protection, anti-piracy, battlefield reconnaissance, and search and rescue.

The squadron that scored the FAA's biggest victory (815 NAS)

Today, 815 NAS is the dedicated front-line squadron for the Wildcat, having sixteen operational flights worldwide plus the Maritime Interdiction flight, which supports counterterrorism operations in the UK. It is also the squadron that crippled the Italian fleet at Taranto in 1940, revolutionising naval warfare and providing the Japanese with the blueprint for their attack on Pearl Harbor a year later.

Black Cats (825 NAS)

The carefully selected aircrew of 825 NAS have extensive experience of test-flying, tactical operations and training, which is why they are charged with introducing new generations of kit to the FAA. Their most recent achievement has been the introduction of the Wildcat into operational service, and they continue to provide the first-class training and procedures required by those who will fly the state-of-the-art helicopter.

The engineers and aircrew of 825 NAS also provide, on a voluntary basis, a Lynx Wildcat display team known as the Black Cats, who perform at air shows around Britain and Europe.

Commando Helicopter Force (845, 846, 847 NAS)

Known as the 'Junglies' since earning the nickname on Borneo in the 1960s, the Commando Helicopter Force (CHF) squadrons today provide support and transportation to 3 Commando Brigade RM, using Lynx Wildcat and Merlin HM Mk3 helicopters. (The main difference between the Merlin Mk3 used by the CHF and the Merlin Mk2 based at Culdrose is that the Mk3 has a rear cargo door.) The CHF squadrons also engage in counterterrorism, anti-piracy and humanitarian operations as required and constitute an important element of Joint Helicopter Command of the British Armed Forces. CHF has three squadrons with very different roles.

- ▶ 845 NAS: A specialist unit flying Merlins to provide troop transport and load-lifting support to 3 Commando Brigade.

- ▶ 846 NAS: Also flying Merlins, 846 NAS supports 3 Commando Brigade in ship-to-shore amphibious assault operations.

- ▶ 847 NAS: Flying the Lynx Wildcat, the primary role of 847 NAS is to provide oversight of the front-line battle space to 3 Commando Brigade.

Note: The twenty-five Merlin Mk3 helicopters of Commando Helicopter Force will be upgraded by 2020 to Merlin Mk4, fully optimised for ship operations and including automatic main rotor blade folding and tail fold. They will enjoy the same fully digital cockpit as the Merlin Mk2, giving the entire Merlin fleet a common feel.

Carry On Flying (727 NAS)
Using general aviation fixed-wing Grob Tutor trainer aircraft, 727 NAS provides advanced flight training and experience for Royal Navy and Royal Marine pilots.

THE DUNKER

The Helicopter Underwater Escape Training Unit, known as the 'Dunker', simulates a helicopter ditching in the sea in different conditions, including in the dark, in rough weather and upside down. All helicopter aircrew and frequent passengers must learn how to escape from a submerged helicopter as part of their training, so the facility is used by all three Armed Forces as well as Air Ambulance, Fire Service, and Search and Rescue crews. Even the chaplains assigned to the FAA must undergo the ordeal of the Dunker, just to prove that they can escape from below the waterline before walking off on top of it.

The Royal Navy Historic Flight

The Royal Navy Historic Flight based at Yeovilton flies vintage Fairey Swordfish biplane torpedo bombers, single-propeller Hawker Sea Fury fighter planes and a Hawker Sea Hawk jet fighter at air shows as a living memorial to all who have served in the Royal Naval Air Service or Fleet Air Arm.

F-35B LIGHTNING II FIGHTER

The STOVL (Short Take-Off and Vertical Landing) capability of the F-35B Lightning II Fighter will allow up to thirty-six of the stealth jets to operate from the Navy's two new supercarriers. They will be flown by the pilots of 809 NAS and the 617 Dambusters Squadron of the RAF, who will be based together at RAF Marham in Norfolk when they are not at sea. In previous incarnations, 809 NAS saw action throughout World War Two and flew Sea Harriers during the Falklands Conflict.

FAA pilots and engineers have been involved from the start in operational trials at Edwards Air Force Base in California and have undergone training at the Eglin Air Force Base in Florida (the aircraft is only made in America).

The F-35B has the following very impressive characteristics.

- ► Its maximum speed is a staggering 1,200 miles per hour.

- ► It has a maximum range of 900 nautical miles (1,036 miles).

- ► Due to its shape and the materials used to build it, it is very difficult to detect, having a radar cross-section the size of a golf ball.

- ► Its sophisticated weaponry includes guided bombs and air-to-surface and air-to-air missiles.

- ► To maintain its low radar profile, it carries its weapons inside the aircraft, although it can also carry air-to-air missiles outside if extra firepower needs to take preference over invisibility to radar.

- ► A panoramic colour display within the cockpit provides all the tactical information and system data required by the pilot, and the pilot's helmet visor provides a head-up display of target information by day and night.

- ► Speech-recognition technology allows the pilot to tell the aircraft what to do.

SQUADRONS BASED AT RAF LOCATIONS

Because it sometimes makes economic and operational sense to share facilities across the Armed Forces, the FAA has two other complete squadrons (in addition to 809 NAS at RAF Marham) stationed on RAF bases.

RAF BARKSTON HEATH (703 NAS)

RAF Barkston Heath in Lincolnshire is home to 703 NAS, which provides Elementary Flying Training for would-be Navy pilots, with successful candidates then being streamed to either helicopter or fast-jet training. The squadron also provides Elementary Observer Training for would-be Navy observers, with successful candidates going on to 750 NAS at Culdrose for more advanced training.

RAF SHAWBURY (705 NAS)

RAF Shawbury in Shropshire is home to 705 NAS, which forms part of the Defence Helicopter Flying School there. All RN rotary pilots undergo their initial six-month helicopter training at Shawbury, including emergency handling, solo flying, engine-off landing, night flying, low-level flying and formation flying. Yes, apparently these are the basics of helicopter flying, after which successful RN candidates go on to learn the 'difficult stuff' with the Fleet Air Arm!

ALL IN A DAY'S WORK

Search and Rescue (SAR)

Until the SRA role was privatised in 2016, the FAA (in conjunction with the RAF) had a proud record of providing search and rescue operations around the coastline of the UK. HMS Gannet at Prestwick Airport in Scotland and 771 NAS at Culdrose deployed helicopters (latterly Sea Kings) every day of the year to help those in distress, saving tens of thousands of lives in the process. The men and women involved in those operations received numerous bravery awards and countless letters of thanks from those whose lives they saved. It goes without saying that the crews of FAA squadrons still provide search and rescue operations for military purposes.

NAVY SPEAK
PILOT TYPES

Once FAA pilots and aircrew have secured their wings (flying badges), they become one of three types of naval flyers: a 'Pinger', a 'Junglie' or a 'Third Pronger'. A Pinger is an Anti-Submarine Warfare (ASW) specialist, the name having originally derived from the pinging sound made by the Sea King's active (dipping) sonar. A 'pinger's moon' is when the skies are clear, the moon is full and the horizon is clearly visible. A Junglie joins one of the Commando Helicopter Force squadrons to transport and support marines in many different environments, including, as the name suggests, in the jungle. A 'Third Pronger', so called on the basis that they haven't joined one of the other two prongs, joins a ship's flight to protect it from attack, amongst other things.

FAMOUS PILOTS

There is something about flying that attracts naturally brave people and cool-headed pioneers and adventurers, and many of them found their way into the Fleet Air Arm at one point or another. Even royals and actors have often found the lure of the open skies too hard to resist. Let's have a look at just some of the great pilots and characters 'made in the FAA'.

VICE ADMIRAL RICHARD BELL DAVIES (1886–1966)

Richard Bell Davies was the first naval aviator to receive the Victoria Cross. While carrying out a bombing raid over Bulgaria during World War One, he landed in marshland to rescue a downed pilot notwithstanding the approach of an enemy party on land. The pilot he rescued was so wedged into the single-seater cockpit of his plane on the way back to base that it took over an hour to extricate him when they got there.

FIGHTER ACE STANLEY ORR (1916–2003)

Although it took him two attempts to pass the eyesight test, Flight Commander Stanley Orr went on to become the Navy's top fighter ace of World War Two, shooting down seventeen enemy aircraft while flying with 806 and 804 NAS. He attacked German shipping and oil facilities in Norway, provided cover for the evacuation of Dunkirk, provided fighter cover at the Battle of Taranto and over Malta, and attacked German positions at Libya and on Rhodes. He also provided fighter cover for the air attack on the German battleship *Tirpitz* off Norway.

COMMANDER CHARLES LAMB (1914–81)

Published in 1977, Charles Lamb's memoirs *To War in a Stringbag* recount his extensive experience as an FAA pilot during World War Two. His operations included mine-laying, U-boat hunting and flying as one of the two Swordfish Pathfinder pilots at the famous Battle of Taranto. He spent a year as a POW in North Africa after his plane got wrecked while landing a secret agent there.

LIEUTENANT LAURENCE OLIVIER (1907–89) AND LIEUTENANT COMMANDER RALPH RICHARDSON (1902–83)

These two great actors took time out to fly in the FAA during World War Two but gained a reputation as 'prangers' given the number of crashes they managed to have. When the tide of the war had turned in 1944, the Old Vic requested their release to re-establish the theatre in London. As Olivier put it at the time, the Sea Lords agreed with 'a speediness and lack of reluctance that was positively hurtful'.

LIEUTENANT COMMANDER ERIC 'WINKLE' BROWN (1919–2016)

Eric 'Winkle' Brown was the FAA's most decorated pilot and the first to land a solely jet-propelled aircraft on to the deck of an aircraft carrier when he touched down on HMS *Ocean* in a modified de Havilland Vampire in December 1945. He held world records for the most types of aircraft flown by an individual (487, including many types of captured German aircraft during World War Two), and the most aircraft carrier landings (2,271) and take-offs (2,407). He became such a household name that he was chosen, at the ripe old age of ninety-five, to appear on the 3,000th edition of *Desert Island Discs* in 2014.

SUB LIEUTENANT BRIAN 'SMOO' ELLIS

'Smoo' Ellis was one of the four 802 NAS pilots flying outdated single-propeller Hawker Sea Fury fighter planes during the Korean War in August 1952 when eight Chinese state-of-the-art MiG jets were spotted and engaged. The superior airmanship of the FAA pilots resulted in Ellis downing one of the MiGs and in three others being severely damaged, whereupon the Sea Furies returned unscathed to their carrier, HMS *Ocean*. Ellis is one of only a few propeller-aircraft pilots to have shot down a jet.

For sixty-five years the 'kill' was wrongly attributed to flight leader Lieutenant Peter 'Hoagy' Carmichael, but *The Times* revealed the true story after Ellis got in touch with them in 2017.

ROYAL FLYERS

Prince Charles qualified as a helicopter pilot at Yeovilton in 1974 (having previously qualified as a fixed-wing pilot with the RAF) and flew with 845 NAS off the carrier HMS *Hermes*. He later put his FAA training to good use in piloting the Wessex helicopters of the Queen's Flight.

Prince Andrew flew as a Sea King pilot with 820 NAS on missions during the Falklands Conflict, including anti-surface and anti-submarine missile operations. He also performed the dangerous task of missile decoy, whereby a helicopter hovers close to a ship to confuse the targeting system of an incoming sea-skimming missile, and was first on the scene to lift casualties from the stricken container ship *Atlantic Conveyor*. He later learned to fly the Lynx and qualified as a Helicopter Warfare Instructor.

THE ROYAL
FLEET AUXILIARY
(RFA)

Since 1905, the civilians of the RFA have been replenishing and supporting the Navy's ships at sea. At that time, sail was giving way to coal-fired steam engines as the primary means of propulsion, meaning that coal had to be delivered along with other vital supplies to ships in overseas ports. Coal gave way to oil during World War One, paving the way for fuel replenishment at sea by the time of World War Two, which became increasingly important as overseas bases were either captured or cut off, and because the Pacific theatre of war in particular was a long way from home.

As the British Empire shrank after World War Two, the Navy found itself with very few permanent overseas bases, which meant the RFA became its main source of support, replenishing fuel and stores during conflicts as far-flung as Korea, Borneo, the Falklands and the Gulf. The RFA played a major part in the Falklands Conflict, during which they lost the RFA *Sir Galahad* (see below).

In 2008, the RFA was presented with a Queen's Colour, their Blue Ensign being proudly embellished with the EiiR cipher, an honour that remains unique to a civilian organisation.

RFA *SIR GALAHAD*

The RFA *Sir Galahad* was a Round Table-class Landing Ship (Logistics) launched in 1966 with the capacity to carry 500 troops, sixteen tanks, thirty-four other vehicles, 122 tonnes of fuel and 31 tonnes of ammunition. She served the British Army until 1970, when she was transferred to the RFA. In late 1970, she took part in the operation to provide humanitarian aid to East Pakistan (now Bangladesh) after it was devastated by a cyclone.

In 1982, she sailed from Devonport as part of the Falklands Task Force, with 350 marines on board. With the marines safely ashore, she was hit in San Carlos Water by a 1,000-pound (450-kilogram) bomb dropped by an Argentinian Skyhawk jet. The bomb was later removed from the ship after it failed to explode. About two weeks later, she was hit by three 500-pound bombs, again dropped from Skyhawks, while preparing to land soldiers of the Welsh Guards in Port Pleasant. This time the bombs exploded, causing the ship to catch fire and killing forty-eight soldiers and crew.

Her captain, Philip Roberts, waited until the last minute to abandon ship and was the last to leave, later being awarded the DSO for his bravery and leadership. Chiu Yiu-Nam, a seaman on board, was awarded the George Medal for rescuing ten men trapped by fire below decks. Guardsman Simon Weston survived the attack with forty-six per cent burns and has gone on to carry out important charity work following the traumas of his much-publicised recovery.

RFA *DILIGENCE*

Another stalwart that saw action during the Falklands Conflict was RFA *Diligence*, a Rig Repair Ship requisitioned by the task force to carry out repairs to the fleet as and when required. Having been bought outright by the RFA in 1984, she went on to win the 'Kuwait 1991' battle honour after providing support to two damaged US ships. With an impressive array of workshops and cranes for hull and machinery repairs, and able to supply fuel, water, electricity, air and steam, she continued to provide repair and maintenance to ships and submarines operating away from their home ports until finally being laid up in 2016.

THE RFA TODAY
The civilian-run vessels of the RFA today continue to act as mother ships around the world, delivering supplies and providing auxiliary services wherever and whenever needed. The primary services delivered by over two thousand RFA personnel are as follows.

- ▶ Logistical support at sea, from replenishment of stores and refuelling to on-the-spot maintenance and repairs for ships and even helicopters.

- ▶ Operational support, including the capability to deliver an amphibious fighting force, along with the vehicles, ammunition and supplies they need.

- ▶ Medical support, through the provision of a Casualty Receiving Ship.

- ▶ Disaster relief and other emergency support, including evacuation, firefighting and first aid.

THE RFA FLEET
At the time of writing, the RFA fleet consisted of the following ships.

- ▶ RFA *Argus*: A casualty receiving ship with a 100-bed medical facility, including resuscitation and surgical facilities, a radiology suite and an intensive-care unit. She also carries Merlin Mk2 helicopters to collect and transfer casualties, and she serves as a helicopter training and repair ship when not required operationally (see below for information about the ship's history).

► Bay-class landing ships: RFA *Mounts Bay*, *Lyme Bay* and *Cardigan Bay* provide significant amphibious capability to the Royal Navy and Royal Marines, able to embark around 350 troops and up to 150 trucks or twenty-four tanks. They each have helicopter landing decks, while *Cardigan Bay* also has the capability to operate as a casualty receiving ship.

► Support ships: RFA *Fort Austin*, *Fort Rosalie* and *Fort Victoria* replenish Navy ships at sea with food, ammunition, explosives and spare parts. They can replenish concurrently from each side, i.e. two ships at a time, and they have helicopter flight decks that allow them to deliver supplies by VERTREP (Vertical Replenishment). *Fort Victoria* also operates as a tanker, able to supply two warships simultaneously with both oil and stores. The ships can support a Royal Marines landing force from the sea. *Fort Austin* took part in the San Carlos landings in the Falklands Conflict as an ammunition ship, and has also served in operations off Sierra Leone, Iraq and Libya.

► Tankers: RFA *Wave Knight* and *Wave Ruler* replenish warships with fuel (including aviation fuel for on-board aircraft), water, dry cargo and refrigerated goods. As evidenced by the 'Naval Service Teamwork' story below, though, they can turn their hands to very different operations when required.

Note: RFA *Tidespring* was due to enter service in late 2017. She is the first of four new Tide-class fast fleet tankers that will ensure the RFA can continue to supply the vessels of the Navy at sea for the foreseeable future. Three more support ships are also planned.

RFA ARGUS

Within a year of being launched as a merchant container ship in 1981, RFA *Argus* was requisitioned for use as a helicopter landing ship during the Falklands Conflict. She was purchased by the RFA in 1984 and converted to an aviation training ship, then converted once more to a casualty receiving ship during the Gulf War in 1991 (because she is armed, she cannot be classified as a hospital ship under the terms of the Geneva Convention).

She has also supported military operations in Bosnia, Kosovo, Sierra Leone and Iraq and, as we have already seen, she was deployed to Sierra Leone again in 2014 to provide aviation support and medical aid in the struggle against the Ebola virus. Using three of her on-board Merlin helicopters, the aircrew of 820 NAS and the marines of 1 Assault Group delivered vital equipment, supplies and food packages from *Argus* to remote areas throughout the country. She enjoyed a well-deserved moment in the limelight in 2011 when she appeared in the film *World War Z* as the fictional assault ship USS *Argus*.

ALL IN A DAY'S WORK

Naval Service teamwork

A great example of the versatility and cohesion of the wider Naval Service was when it brought about the capture of drug runners in the Caribbean in November 2016. Responding to a call to intercept a speedboat travelling between Venezuela and Puerto Rico, the RFA's fast tanker RFA *Wave Knight* bore down on the target and launched her on-board Lynx helicopter from 815 NAS with a Royal Marine sniper on board. After the sniper's warning shots across the speedboat's bow were ignored, he took out the speedboat's engines with precision firing from on high, bringing the vessel to a halt. When the US Coast Guard boarded the speedboat, they assessed the haul at £40 million worth of cocaine. The simultaneous deployment of the FAA, the Marines, the RFA and the US Coast Guard got the job done quickly and efficiently. That's what you call teamwork.

OTHER NAVY SERVICES AND RESERVES

The five regular arms of the Navy are underpinned by the Maritime Reserves and by a number of essential full-time services, including the provision of marine services, medical support, logistics, engineering and policing.

THE MARITIME RESERVES

The Maritime Reserves must be maintained at a constant state of readiness, so that they can be called upon at times of stretch, tension, crisis or war. They are made up of the Royal Naval Reserve (RNR) and the Royal Marines Reserve (RMR), each of which offer meaningful careers to individuals who have what it takes to switch regularly between their civilian jobs and their military responsibilities. It is not unusual for ex-regular personnel to join the Reserves, and it is great news when they do, because they come ready trained and with invaluable operational experience under their belt. The Maritime Reserves provide around ten per cent of the total workforce of the Naval Service, and at the time of writing there are around 3,000 RNR and 750 RMR reservists.

The Royal Naval Reserve (RNR)

Often indistinguishable from their regular counterparts, those serving in the RNR over the years have seen action around the globe, including during the two world wars, the Iraq War and the war in Afghanistan. In more recent times, they have been involved in operations as diverse as counterterrorism and anti-piracy in the Gulf.

There are currently eighteen units around the country, who each ensure that their reservists get all the training and experience they need to remain fit and able for action at short notice.

- ▶ HMS Calliope, Tyneside

- ▶ HMS Cambria, Cardiff

- ▶ HMS Ceres, Leeds

- ▶ HMS Dalriada, Glasgow

- ▶ HMS Eaglet, Liverpool

- ▶ HMS Ferret, Bedford (home to the RNR Intelligence Branch, who have supported operations in many theatres of war, including the Balkans, Iraq and Afghanistan)

- ▶ HMS Flying Fox, Bristol

- ▶ HMS Forward, Birmingham

- ▶ Hawke Division, Medway

- ▶ HMS Hibernia, Belfast

- ▶ HMS King Alfred, Portsmouth (one of the largest Reserve units in the country, perhaps not surprising given its situation in the

heart of a naval city, with regular opportunities to experience the
Navy first-hand and make use of the excellent facilities there)

► HMS President, London (downstream of Tower Bridge)

► HMS Scotia, Rosyth

► HMS Sherwood, Nottingham (a thriving unit for over fifty
years despite being located 50 miles from the nearest coastline)

► Tawe Division, Swansea

► Tay Division, Dundee

► HMS Vivid, Plymouth (another unit to benefit from its situation
on a naval base, in this case the largest one in Western Europe
at HMNB Devonport, with all the opportunities that entails)

► HMS Wildfire, Northwood (like HMS Sherwood, a unit that
has flown the White Ensign for over fifty years despite being
50 miles from the nearest saltwater)

In addition to these eighteen units, there is an RNR Air Branch, open
only to ex-regulars and those who have significant maritime aviation
experience. As the branch covers all trades and specialisations of the
Fleet Air Arm, including flying, reservists can be attached to any
FAA squadron or unit around the country.

The Royal Marines Reserve (RMR)

RMR Marines must complete the same commando course as their
regular counterparts to secure the coveted green beret and serve on
front-line amphibious operations. Although the 600 or so reserves
serve part-time in parallel with their civilian careers, they must be
ready to be deployed at any time and to go wherever in the world
they are needed for military or humanitarian purposes.

There are four RMR units with multiple detachments around the country, all of which maintain the infantry, amphibious, cold-weather warfare and commando skills of the regular Marines. After a few years as a General Duties Rifleman, they can choose one of four specialisations: Landing Craft Coxswain, Assault Engineer, Heavy Weapons (Mortars) or Swimmer Canoeist.

- ▶ RMR Bristol, with detachments at Poole, Plymouth, Cardiff and Lympstone.

- ▶ RMR London, with detachments at Cambridge, Henley and Portsmouth.

- ▶ RMR Merseyside, in Liverpool, with detachments at Manchester, Birmingham, Nottingham and Leeds.

- ▶ RMR Scotland, in Rosyth, with detachments at Aberdeen, Belfast, Dundee, Edinburgh, Glasgow and Newcastle (RMR Scotland, of course, has an environmental advantage when it comes to learning cold-weather warfare).

ALL IN A DAY'S WORK

Lance Corporal Matthew Croucher (1983–)

It is estimated that sixty per cent of RMR Reserves at any one time have served on combat operations, and many have done tours in Iraq and Afghanistan in recent times. They include Lance Corporal Matthew Croucher, who was awarded the George Cross while serving with 40 Commando in Afghanistan in 2008. When entering a compound, he felt a grenade tripwire activate, whereupon he immediately fell on the device to protect his colleagues from the blast. His bergen and body armour cushioned much of the explosion, leaving him with only minor injuries.

THE SEA CADET CORPS

The Sea Cadet Corps is a maritime youth charity teaching life skills through nautical adventures. Its origins date back to the Crimean War, when sailors returning home set up Naval Lads' Brigades to help orphans in the backstreets of seaports around the country. Queen Victoria donated £10 for the Windsor Unit to purchase uniforms for the first time in 1899, and in 1919 the thirty-four brigades of the time gained Admiralty recognition and the title of (Navy League) Sea Cadet Corps. Girls have been admitted since 1980 and some units also have a Royal Marines Cadet detachment.

Cadets receive rigorous training, including hands-on experience on board many different boats and ships, and they can specialise in areas such as seamanship, marine engineering, navigation or communications. Although there is no direct pathway from the Sea Cadets into the Royal Navy or Royal Marines, many cadets do make that step up of their own accord. Around 14,000 young people belong to around 400 units across the UK today, supported by around 9,000 volunteers.

THE ROYAL NAVY MEDICAL SERVICE

Ever since treatment for sick and wounded naval personnel was administered by the Commissioners of the Sick and Hurt Board from 1692 onwards, surgeons and other medical staff have been saving lives and treating injuries and disease on sea and land. Today the 1,500 or so personnel of the Navy's Medical Service continue to look after the Navy's most valuable asset – the people who serve in its ranks.

As their duties include running the on-board sick bay, attending to diving-related injuries, dealing with radiation exposure and delivering primary care in the heart of the action in a conflict zone, Medical Assistants receive similar training to paramedics. Whether on board ships or submarines or in field hospitals near the front line, they attend to all types of injuries, illnesses and diseases – sometimes when their patients may also be their friends.

Today's pop-up field hospitals and on-board operating theatres have the advantage of state-of-the-art equipment and anaesthetics, a far cry from the rudimentary surgical saws and swig of rum used on board the sailing ships of old. It's also fairly certain that the sailors of Nelson's Navy didn't enjoy the benefits of environmental health and safety, radiography, hygienic dentistry, mental health care or biomedical science, all of which play their part in keeping the Navy of today happy, healthy and wise.

ALL IN A DAY'S WORK

Surgeon-Captain Rick Jolly (1946–)

Rick Jolly's twenty-four years of service included serving as Medical Officer to 42 Commando in Northern Ireland and two tours as Fleet Surgeon to the Fleet Air Arm. As Senior Medical Officer of 3 Commando Brigade, he commanded the field hospital at Ajax Bay during the Falklands Conflict. Conditions at the hospital were poor, and Jolly and his team faced a constant struggle amidst dim lighting, dirt, air attacks and two resident unexploded bombs. Not one of the hundreds of British and Argentinian troops under his care died of their wounds, and he later achieved the unique distinction of being decorated by both the British and Argentinian governments for his efforts.

'Doc' Jolly went on to write an account of his Falklands experience in *Doctor for Friend and Foe* and also spent decades putting together the much-acclaimed *Jackspeak*, a comprehensive explanation of around 4,000 terms of Navy slang (first published in 1989 and twice updated since then).

QUEEN ALEXANDRA'S ROYAL NAVAL NURSING SERVICE (QARNNS)

Ever since the first nursing sisters were despatched to the Crimea in 1854, the Navy's Nursing Service has been working alongside its medical teams at home and abroad. Today the three hundred or so nurses of the QARNNS perform a wide range of tasks, either to meet operational needs or to provide disaster relief or humanitarian assistance. Their field operations include support to 3 Commando Brigade as the Commando Surgical Forward Group, and they also deliver surgical and other emergency procedures on board HMS *Argus*, the RFA's casualty receiving ship.

The considerable skills of the Nursing Service, many of which necessarily overlap with those of the Medical Service, enable the following vital interventions.

► Damage control resuscitation, which is urgent surgical intervention to prevent haemorrhaging and limit contamination prior to more definitive surgery.

► Intensive care, including respiratory, circulatory and renal support.

► Blood transfusions.

► Immediate treatment of burns.

► Life-, limb- and eye-saving surgery or other care.

▶ Administering of anaesthetics.

▶ Prevention and control of infection.

▶ Wound care.

▶ Trauma control.

A BRIEF HISTORY OF THE NAVY'S NURSING SERVICE

1854:   During the Crimean War, the Navy set up a hospital at the naval base near Constantinople and despatched six nursing sisters to work there alongside the traditionally male medical staff.

1879:   The Navy sent six nurses from the Royal Victoria Hospital at Netley near Southampton to work in South Africa during the Anglo-Zulu War.

1884:   The uniformed, officer-only Naval Nursing Service was born, initially to staff the naval hospitals at Haslar, near Gosport, and Plymouth, although steps were taken to ensure that the female nurses never saw more than the heads, shoulders and feet of the male patients (only male medical staff could be trusted to do that without losing control of their senses).

1885:   Sisters from the Naval Nursing Service were stationed on hospital ships in the Red Sea to tend to sailors and marines fighting in the Sudan Campaign. Another group of naval nurses went up the Nile with the Army's ill-fated expedition to relieve Khartoum.

1902:   Queen Alexandra became President of the Nursing Staff, and the service was renamed in her honour.

1914:   The service was significantly expanded at the outbreak of World War One, and many nurses were deployed overseas during both world wars.

1959:   Auxiliary nursing roles were introduced, thereby creating opportunities for ratings to work in the service alongside officers.

1982:   Forty QARNNS personnel served on the hospital ship SS *Uganda* during the Falklands Conflict.

1983:   The service opened its door to male nurses.

2000–:   Twenty-first-century deployments have included Iraq, Afghanistan, Sierra Leone (to combat the Ebola virus) and the Mediterranean (e.g. to administer to migrants who had been stranded at sea).

THE ROYAL NAVY CHAPLAINCY SERVICE

The RN Chaplaincy Service provides clergy from different denominations to give pastoral and spiritual care to the men and women of the Naval Service and their dependants. They serve in times of peace and conflict in all kinds of places around the world, at sea or on land. Unlike in the Army and RAF, they wear no badges of rank, so they share the rank of the person they are talking to at any point in time, from rear admiral or major general to able rate or marine.

THE ROYAL NAVY POLICE (RNP)

Formerly known as the Regulating Branch, the RNP is the police branch of both the Royal Navy and Royal Marines. Although they no longer have to check that the ship's lanterns are out at night or present prisoners for flogging, they do have far-reaching responsibilities, including global criminal investigation (such as cybercrime) and counternarcotics and anti-piracy operations at sea. More routinely, they are responsible for maintaining discipline on naval bases or on board ships.

THE ROYAL NAVY LOGISTICS BRANCH
The Logistics Branch is what keeps the Navy ticking, whether as chefs, stewards or HR administrators (called 'writers') on board, or as supply-chain specialists responsible for the worldwide delivery of vital stores and equipment. On-board teams are led by their Logistics Officer, who has responsibility for managing everything six months ahead, including the movement of personnel, the delivery and management of operational supplies (food, ammunition, fuel, linen, you name it) or even humanitarian aid.

THE ROYAL NAVY ENGINEERING BRANCH
The Engineering Branch literally keeps the Navy moving and, when necessary, fighting. Its engineers are responsible for the smooth running of ships, submarines and aircraft, which means they must know how to fix things wherever and whenever they need fixing. They provide specialists in many types of engineering, from weapons to communications, from helicopters to nuclear propulsion. Maintenance is constant, because it's a bit late to find out that you can't engage third gear when you're chasing down pirates or gunrunners on the high seas.

THE MARINE SERVICES
Largely operating out of the naval bases at Portsmouth, Devonport and Clyde, Marine Services (provided by Serco Group at the time of writing) provide support at home and abroad to the Navy, Marines and RFA, using tugs, tenders and ship-borne heavy-lifting equipment.

The port services they provide include the towing, berthing and loading of ships and submarines, the transfer of crew to and from vessels, the maintenance of navigational buoys and moorings, and the storage of munitions. Out-of-port services include the support of training operations, including diving, mine laying and the towing of targets to be used in artillery or torpedo exercises. Overseas services involve similar port and out-of-port operations in locations such as Gibraltar and the Falklands.

Marine Services have around a hundred vessels at their disposal, including SD *Northern River*, which is large enough to transport the NATO Submarine Rescue System to the location of a distressed submarine.

PART THREE

THE PEOPLE, CULTURE AND TRADITIONS OF THE NAVY

Equipment has its place, but our future will be governed as much by the attitude, optimism, creativity and confidence of the men and women who have chosen to pursue a career in the Naval Service.

SIR GEORGE ZAMBELLAS, FORMER FIRST SEA LORD

LIFE AT SEA

There is an adage that goes: 'A sailor lives where he fights; a soldier fights where he lives.' That remains largely true today, but life at sea on a modern ship or submarine is rather different to the life experienced on the Navy's wooden sailing ships of old. That was a time when mutiny, scurvy, tropical diseases, lashes of the whip, weevil-infested food and cramped, filthy living conditions were as much concerns as enemy cannonballs and the brutal hand-to-hand fighting that often took place in the middle of a sea battle. In this chapter, we will look at life at sea then and now for the sailors of the Royal Navy.

NELSON'S NAVY

The food staples below deck during Nelson's time were oatmeal, salted meat and fish, hard biscuit, peas, cheese, butter, flour, raisins, oatmeal beer and half a pint of watered-down rum. On the upside, that was better than most people back on land were getting at the time.

British sailors shared their life on board with many other nationalities, something which must have been a bit of an eye-opener in the days when global travel was not otherwise possible and Britain didn't enjoy much in the way of inbound tourism.

There were seventy-one foreign sailors on board *Victory* at Trafalgar, including twenty-three Americans and four Frenchmen (probably captured in a previous battle). There would have been pets on board to keep the sailors amused, the favourites being cats, dogs and parrots (and a mongoose if possible, to take care of the cockroaches and rats). The practice of keeping on-board pets was not banned until the 1970s, when the health and safety people finally got their way.

NAVY SPEAK

Some terms that later found their way into modern-day English had their origins in the galleys of Nelson's Navy.

SQUARE MEAL
Now meaning 'all you need to survive on a single plate', the 'square meal' derived from the fact that the wooden dinner plates on sailing ships were square-shaped, presumably to stop them rolling away when the going got rough.

PIPING HOT
We all know that this is the perfect temperature to serve hot food at, and so it was in Nelson's time. If you collected your food from the galley as soon as the appropriate pipe had sounded (nowadays it is more likely to be a tannoy announcement), it was said to be 'piping hot'.

ON THE FIDDLE
The edge that ran around all four sides of the square wooden plates used on sailing ships was called a 'fiddle'. If you served yourself so much food that it touched the sides of your plate, you were said to be 'on the fiddle', which remains a common term today for taking something you're not entitled to.

SLUSH FUND

Nowadays referring to excess funds set aside for a rainy day, 'slush' was originally the term for fat skimmed off the cauldrons of boiled meat in a ship's galley. The chef would compact the slush and sell it to the purser to turn into candles, thus setting up a nice little 'slush fund' from the proceeds.

Battle conditions in Nelson's Navy

The battle conditions in Nelson's Navy were nothing short of horrific. Below deck, round shot beheaded sailors and cut heavy cannons loose to roll about. Above deck, cannonballs linked with chain or bars scythed through masts, yards, rigging and, of course, sailors. Canister and grapeshot sprayed metal pieces everywhere and wooden splinters caused by cannon shot caused as many deaths as anything. Long splinters travelling nearly as fast as shot itself could slice through and disembowel any sailor standing in the wrong place at the wrong time. The Battle of Trafalgar was not won by sinking ships; it was won by killing more men in these horrific ways than the French managed in return.

Not all wounds on board sailing warships were inflicted by the enemy. The use of gunpowder – a combination of saltpetre, charcoal and sulphur so volatile that it had to be mixed wet in the first place – caused many a powder burn and lost limb to those who carried it to the gun decks or loaded it into the guns.

As if all that wasn't bad enough, sailors also had to suffer the humiliation of taking orders from midshipmen as young as eleven. The youngest officer on board *Victory* at Trafalgar was just twelve, but many of these boys fought and died as bravely as their 'Jack Tars'.

The human cost of sea battles was immense, but for those that survived their injuries (lost limbs and permanent deafness were both common) there was at least a pension waiting upon presentation of their Hurt Certificate, which described the wound in question.

Women on board

To prevent sailors in Nelson's Navy absconding in the eighteenth century when anchored near land, Navy boatmen would be sent ashore to bring out wives to those sailors who had one in that particular port, or prostitutes to those that didn't. Wives and daughters were also taken to sea unofficially, spending their days cooking, washing, cleaning and sewing in return for the 'privilege' of sharing the food ration and hammock of their husband or father. As the Navy needed all the help it could get going into a sea battle, women were not excluded then either. They carried gunpowder to the gun decks and helped surgeons treat the wounded.

NAVY SPEAK

SON OF A GUN

It was not uncommon for children to be conceived or born on board Navy warships in Nelson's time – most likely between the cannons of a gun deck, because that was where sailors and their families also slept. The phrase used to describe a child born on board at the time was 'son of a gun', which survives in a wider sense to this day to describe 'a bit of a character'.

COLD ENOUGH TO FREEZE THE BALLS OFF A BRASS MONKEY

In a naval context, this happened when it got cold enough for iron cannonballs to contract and fall through the holes of the brass storage tracks (monkeys) that held them in place alongside the cannons on the fighting decks of sailing warships.

MUTINIES

Sometimes life just got too much for the Navy's sailors, which was hardly surprising given the injustices of their pay and conditions and the brutality of the disciplinary regime they were subjected to in the past.

Not all mutinies were caused by injustice, though. As we have seen, the crew of the Tudor flagship *Grace Dieu* refused to sail because they objected to having soldiers and archers on board, while the English Civil War saw men mutiny in support of the Royalist cause. In the 1740s many crew members mutinied while on Admiral Anson's circumnavigation of the globe, but it was either that or die of scurvy like so many others did on that voyage. Even the most famous mutiny of all, that on HMS *Bounty* in 1789, probably had more to do with half the crew deciding that life on a Pacific island with an exotic native girl was rather more fun than the quality of life they enjoyed back home in Blighty.

In 1797, rebels with a cause mutinied at Spithead, off Portsmouth, and at Nore, in the Thames estuary, in pursuit of better pay and living conditions, more shore leave, compensation for sickness and injury, and a lessening of the strict disciplinary regime. One 'Punishment Book' of the time refers to a boy receiving an inhumane 250 lashes for insubordination. Other mutinies followed as class solidarity gained momentum and eventually resulted in a gradual improvement in sailors' lives.

The Admiralty got things horribly wrong in 1931, when they backdated a ten per cent pay cut (imposed by the government in accordance with the austerity measures of the Great Depression) in such a way that it led to a twenty-five per cent pay cut for some of the most junior grades. The Invergordon Mutiny was the result, as 1,000 sailors of the British Atlantic Fleet in the Cromarty Firth went on strike. They remained respectful to their officers but caused panic in the London Stock Exchange. The strike ended when the Admiralty recognised their own foolishness and imposed a ten per cent cut across the board.

CAST ADRIFT

Life on board a Navy ship in the eighteenth century may have been tough, but it was nothing compared to being cast adrift on a 23-foot open boat in the middle of the ocean. With no navigation charts, hardly any food and only two weeks' supply of water, Captain William Bligh and eighteen loyal *Bounty* crew were cast adrift near Tonga by Fletcher Christian. They should have perished from starvation or dehydration, but they didn't. Bligh's expert seamanship (having only a sextant and a pocket watch to navigate by) and determination to survive against the odds brought them, barely alive, to the safety of the Dutch East Indies. Their arduous journey of 3,500 nautical miles had taken them almost six weeks.

NAVY SPEAK
TOE THE LINE

When sailors weren't involved in mutinies, they were toeing the line. Whenever a ship's company was mustered for pay or victuals, each sailor stepped forward to a line marked on the deck to give their name and place of duty on the ship, thereby acknowledging authority and obeying the rules, which remains the meaning of the term 'toeing the line' to this day.

VICTORIA'S NAVY

During the Victorian age, there was increasing concern about the welfare of seamen, resulting in increased rations and a greater variety of foods. The beer ration gave way to rum altogether, as rum was easier to store and keep from spoiling, and by 1850 canned meat provided safer foodstuffs on long voyages. By the end of Victoria's reign, fresh bread was being baked on board.

Smokeless, less-volatile cordite finally replaced gunpowder to propel everything from bullets to the heavy armour-piercing shells fired from the Navy's warships. Long, rifled, cast-iron barrels that could be breech-loaded improved distance and accuracy, and gun turrets provided movement and an element of protection to gun crews.

THE RUM RATION

Until after the Napoleonic Wars, the daily alcohol ration for sailors in the Navy had been eight pints of beer, which not only kept morale up but also provided most of the calories they needed. Wine or spirits would be substituted whenever the beer had run out and spirits in particular were easier to store in any event, leading ultimately to the daily ration becoming half a pint of neat rum in place of beer.

The practice of diluting the rum was introduced in the 1740s by Admiral Edward Vernon, known as Old Grog on account of the grogram (ribbed fabric) cloak he wore and thereby giving the drink its nickname of 'grog'.

The rum was diluted more and more until the practice of handing out tots was finally abolished in 1970 for fear that sailors might fail a breathalyser test or not be fully capable of handling increasingly complex machinery and systems. The final rum ration was handed out to sailors at sea on 31 July 1970, which became known as Black Tot Day after sailors conducted mock funerals or threw their tots into the sea in protest. Having turned full circle, a limited amount of beer can be purchased on board ships today, although a tot of rum is still issued on special occasions or to recognise good service (as we have already seen, this is known as 'splicing the main brace').

NAVY SPEAK

THE PUSSER AND HIS RUM

'Pusser' is both a nickname for the Navy and the alternative title of a ship or establishment's Supply Officer, originally known as the 'purser'. Pusser's rum related to the stocks of Admiralty rum that were stored in stone-and-wickerwork jars and supplied to ships on setting sail.

WHEN THE SUN IS OVER THE YARDARM

This Navy term means it is time for the first alcoholic drink of the day, deriving from the fact that the first beer or tot of rum was handed out on sailing ships when the sun rose above the yardarm at the end of the topmost spar of the main mast (around noon on the equator and around 11 a.m. in the North Atlantic).

THE TWENTIETH-CENTURY NAVY

Civilisation crept on board in 1910 when crockery and cutlery were no longer just used by officers. As the century wore on, frozen and dehydrated goods combined with canned foods in allowing longer spells away from port and in securing improvements to food hygiene, but conditions remained cramped on board ships and submarines, and it was difficult to keep your clothes and other belongings anything but wet.

Battle conditions at sea changed dramatically in the first half of the century, requiring the manning of the heavy naval guns that pounded away during the world wars, the rapid firing of anti-aircraft guns like the Bofors and the dropping of depth charges in the hope of disarming or sinking submarines.

The second half of the century brought guided missiles like the surface-to-air Seacat, Sea Slug and Sea Dart used during the Falklands Conflict; the supersonic Sea Wolf, capable of destroying something the size of a cricket ball travelling at three times the speed of sound; and the Harpoon anti-ship missile. Submariners got to grips with increasingly effective torpedoes, like the Spearfish that can be used against ships or submarines of any size, and the land-attack Tomahawk and nuclear-armed Polaris and Trident missiles.

THE NAVY OF TODAY

The Navy today may have a smaller fleet of vessels and fewer people than in days of yore, but it has at its disposal more versatile and agile vessels than ever before. Having a workforce that can react to ever-changing technology, circumstances and demands is equally important.

The food and lodgings enjoyed on board today are a far cry from Nelson's Navy, with individual toilets ('heads') and showers taken for granted and not a single mongoose required to keep the rat population down, but those serving at sea do still face danger and do still need to leave their friends and families behind for long periods.

Let's look at life afloat on a warship, using HMS *Dragon* as our example, and at the somewhat different life experienced on board a submarine.

HMS DRAGON

The first great thing about HMS *Dragon* is that you can't mistake her for any of the Navy's other five Daring-class destroyers. Just look for the one with the huge red dragon emblazoned on the bow of the ship.

Once on board, it's surprising how spacious everything is. This is because the hull had to be made larger than would otherwise have been necessary in order to support the huge tower that holds the radar system aloft (the tower is about the same height as Nelson's Column in Trafalgar Square, which is appropriate for this ultra-modern version of the ships that fought at the Battle of Trafalgar). All this space allows for larger mess rooms to relax in, sleeping quarters that almost resemble Travelodge rooms and a spacious gym to work out in between watches. Even after allowing for all that, there is still room to spare – if every one of the 190 ship's company brought their cats on board, there would be room to swing them all.

The crew enjoy meals prepared in a modern galley that wouldn't look out of place in the better hotels back on shore, have a choice of three main courses for lunch and dinner, and are well catered for even if they have allergies or aversions. They also quickly realise the importance of their laundry supremo, who single-handedly provides a same-day service on uniforms to keep everyone looking spick and span. The laundryman on *Dragon* when I was on board was Dal Bahdar Thapa, who just happened to have served previously as a Gurkha for fifteen years in Burma (Myanmar), Hong Kong, Belize and Britain, so perhaps it's not that surprising that he can perform the relatively simpler task of keeping an entire ship's company looking good.

In addition to the camaraderie and team spirit promised in the Navy Careers Office, there is also an increasing feeling these days that life on board is in many ways ahead of society in general. In 2016, the Royal Navy was elevated to a top ten British employer in the Workplace Equality Index, which may have something to do with the fact that nothing less than total respect for each other will do over long periods at sea, especially under arduous and hostile conditions.

Communication with family and friends back home is not so difficult in these days of email and social media, even allowing for those times when 'silence' is required for operational reasons. It helps to know what's going on at home and to know that you have the support of those you left behind, and that they in turn know that you're safe and being so well fed on a nutritious, balanced diet that their chances of catching scurvy are probably greater than yours.

Turning to the business end of things, there is a 180-degree panoramic view to be enjoyed from the bridge for those assigned to a role that is essential to the driving of the ship. This is not just nice – we all like to see a bit of sky around us – it is also useful, because, as Captain Craig Wood pointed out to me on the bridge of *Dragon*, sometimes it does no harm to take your eyes off the impressive array of instrument panels and just look outside for a moment to get a proper feel for where you are in the world and what the weather is doing out there. There is a particularly fine view to be had from Captain Wood's custom-made 'driving seat', which in a previous life looked just as splendid as the driving seat in a Rolls-Royce Phantom, complete with walnut panelling – well, there have to be some perks to driving a warship!

In the operations room, the key players are grouped together so that during the heat of battle they can communicate with one another in the old-fashioned human methods of speech, hearing, hand signals and body language in addition to focusing on their own individual instrument panels, all of which are a vital part of the coordinated Combat Management System. It feels a bit like the trading floor of the London Stock Exchange, where the traders with the coolest heads under pressure invariably strike the best deals – except that the stakes in this trading room are somewhat higher.

LIFE ON BOARD A SUBMARINE

There is no denying that space remains limited on a submarine compared to a destroyer, but life on board has come a long way since the world wars, when everything, including getting into a hammock, was a bit of a tight fit to say the least and submariners stank permanently of diesel, cabbage and sweat. Every spare inch of today's huge submarines is used to create as much gym and mess space as possible.

The Vanguard-class submarine has a crew of up to 130 spread over three decks that run the 150 metres of the vessel's length. Much-improved domestic facilities and food quality help maintain morale over long periods submerged below the world's oceans, while the purified air and fresh water produced by the on-board nuclear plant makes life much more comfortable than hitherto. Because the location of our submarines must remain top secret over long periods of time, however, telephone and internet access remain very much restricted.

The Dreadnought-class submarines due to replace the Vanguards from 2030 onwards will be bigger again. They will be the first RN submarines to have separate crew quarters, washing facilities and toilets for female submariners, and they will have innovative lighting, which will enable the simulation of night and day.

CHRISTMAS AT SEA

Around one eighth of those who serve at sea remain deployed over Christmas and New Year, while the other seven-eighths undertake a mass migration to their homes and families. On Christmas Day 2016, this meant that 700 crew had to be served Christmas dinner on board the carrier HMS *Ocean*. As it is a Navy tradition that officers serve the crew on Christmas Day, the officers on board *Ocean* had to do so over four sittings lasting more than four hours, following which they also had to wash up 700 sets of plates and cutlery. On some ships, it is also a tradition for the youngest or most junior member of the ship's company to be made captain for Christmas Day.

One small consolation for missing Christmas at home is that ship-based personnel are allowed an extra 30 minutes to call home over the festive period, which doubles the normal weekly allowance of ship-to-shore communication.

DOWNTIME

Shore leave in the far-flung corners of the world is one of the reasons that many join the Navy in the first place, allowing some unique opportunities for sport, adventure and sightseeing.

At sea, notwithstanding the more universal appeal of the iPad these days, the traditional Navy board game of Uckers is still played in the mess room (it's a form of ludo, but with more complex rules and a lot more grandstanding). Other 'indoor' pastimes include reading, watching downloaded films and catching up on favourite TV programmes supplied by the British Forces Broadcasting Service (BFBS).

Outdoors on deck, a game of bucketball helps to pass the time and keep the crew fit while they're about it. It's a fast-paced game using balls made from rags and masking tape to prevent them going over the side too often, with the balls having to be thrown into a bucket held by a member of your own team to achieve a score. It has been described as 'angry netball with moving goalposts'.

Submariners cannot enjoy the output of the BFBS, but they too have access to books (electronic and traditional), DVDs, game consoles and downloaded films. Many make use of their downtime to study on distance-learning courses like those offered by the Open University (as do many ship personnel). They also make their own fun with bingo and quiz nights and, of course, Uckers.

WOMEN IN
THE NAVY

The Royal Navy today has female pilots, submariners, warfare officers, mine-clearance divers, engineers, navigators and much more besides, and they enjoy the same opportunities and face the same levels of danger as the men do. Women now account for around ten per cent of the combined personnel of the Royal Navy and Royal Marines, including at officer level. Thirteen per cent of the ship's company of the new aircraft carrier *Queen Elizabeth* are female, represented at every rank and rate and in every department.

All this is a far cry from the time women put to sea 'unofficially' in the wooden sailing ships of the eighteenth and nineteenth centuries, often disguised as men in their determination to live a less restricted life and see the world. This chapter celebrates the highlights and achievements of women in the Navy over a much longer period than most people might think.

PIONEERS

With the earliest recorded instance dating back to 1690, women who went to sea as men on sailing ships included: Mary Lacy, who served for twelve years as William Chandler without arousing suspicion; a young black woman who joined a ship in Grenada as William Brown, only to be dismissed a month later for the offence of 'being female'; Hannah Snell, the woman who used the name of her brother-in-law James Gray to enlist and fight in the Marines; and Ann Perriam, the wife who served alongside her husband during the sea battles of the Napoleonic Wars. (See below for more information about Hannah Snell and Ann Perriam.)

It may seem staggering to us now, but back in these days medical checks were generally considered a hindrance to recruitment and sailors only rarely undressed or washed. More difficult would have been the occasional need to hide bumps to the fore while receiving lashes of the whip to the aft, and possibly developing the art of standing up at one's toilet.

THE SECRET MARINE

Hannah Snell (1723–92) disguised herself as a man to enlist and fight in the Marines, seeing action during the capture of Pondicherry in India, when she was reported to have received eleven musket-ball wounds to the legs and one to the groin. Either she removed the one from the groin herself or had it removed by a sympathetic Indian doctor in order to preserve her secret. In any event, she revealed her sex on her return to Britain, where she petitioned for an honourable discharge and a military pension.

The Gentlemen's Magazine told her story, which was also published as a book titled *The Female Soldier*. She appeared on stage in her uniform, performing military drills while singing, and three painters made portraits of her in her uniform. The widespread publicity resulted in the Royal Hospital

Chelsea recognising her service, awarding her a pension and ultimately allowing her burial in their military cemetery.

Her story has been told more fully in *Hannah Snell: The Secret Life of a Female Marine* by Matthew Stephens.

NOT MALE ENOUGH

Ann 'Nancy' Perriam went to sea with her first husband, sailor Edward Hopping, in 1785 and took part in several sea battles of the French Revolutionary and Napoleonic Wars, including the Battles of Cape St Vincent and the Nile. The written record she kept tells us that her duties included preparing flannel cartridges for the cannons, assisting the surgeon as he treated the wounded and mending the captain's clothes. The Navy later refused her request for a General Service Medal, a bit of an affront considering they did award one to somebody's baby born during the Battle of the Glorious First of June (but only because it was a male baby – female babies didn't qualify any more than female sailors). She was, however, awarded a Navy pension and lived to the ripe old age of ninety-three on it.

WORLD WAR ONE

In 1914, Katherine Furse led volunteers from the Red Cross and St John's Ambulance Service to France as a Voluntary Aid Detachment (VAD). Her success led in 1917 to her being offered the post of Director of the newly formed WRNS, which quickly amassed 3,000 members. The recruitment posters encouraged women to 'Free a man for sea service' and they undertook a wide range of home-based and overseas duties in over a hundred different roles, including the following.

- ▶ Intelligence officer

- ▶ Wireless telegraphist

- ▶ Operational planner

- ▶ Despatch rider

- ▶ Radar plotter

- ▶ Weapons analyst

- ▶ Range assessor

- ▶ Electrician

- ▶ Air mechanic

- ▶ Sailmaker

- ▶ Cook

- ▶ Steward

In 1918, nineteen-year-old Josephine Carr from Cork became the first Wren to die in active service when her Royal Mail Ship *Leinster* was torpedoed in the Irish Sea by a U-boat.

By the time the service was disbanded in 1919, it had 7,000 members, including 500 officers, and the Navy had paved the way by becoming the first of the three services to recruit women.

NAVY SPEAK
JENNY (OR JENNY WREN)

'Jenny' became the nickname for female sailors in the Navy because members of the WRNS were referred to as 'Wrens' and there is a Dickens character by the name of Jenny Wren in *Our Mutual Friend*.

WORLD WAR TWO

When the WRNS reformed in 1939, they needed additional skills to keep pace with developing technology and more modern warfare methods. Women now performed roles as varied as meteorologist and cryptologist. Some even served at sea, as cipher officers and coders. Others literally took their jobs to new heights by performing airborne duties as reconnaissance photographers or radio operators.

FLYING WREN
The first Wren to fly as part of her regular duties was twenty-one-year-old radio mechanic Lead Wren Pat Lees, who started flying in 755 Squadron Lysanders in 1942.

PLOTTING FOR D-DAY
For the tense few weeks leading up to D-Day, the Wrens who served as weather forecasters and meteorological plotters while hidden

in a hut in the grounds of Southwick House played a crucial role in determining the timing of the Normandy landings. Acting on information received from weather stations and ships, they forecast severe storms for 5 June, resulting in the decision to delay the invasion until the following day.

Wrens also worked as teleprinters in the cellars of Southwick House itself, including Laura Mountney, who would go on to become the world-famous fashion designer Laura Ashley. Twenty of the teleprinters, including Mountney, were picked to travel with the invasion force through Europe after the D-Day landings.

D-DAY

Many Wrens piloted harbour launches and tugs throughout the war, and some took smaller ships across the Channel on D-Day. As Operation NEPTUNE wore on, they towed disabled vessels back to home ports for repairs, which were often carried out by WRNS mechanics.

CODEBREAKERS

Wrens with language skills were used at coastal stations around the country to intercept and translate enemy signals, while some worked at Bletchley Park to help break German and Japanese codes.

The WRNS had 74,000 personnel by 1944, by which time they were doing over 200 different jobs at home and abroad, including in Gibraltar, Singapore, Alexandria, Washington, South Africa and India.

By the end of the war, over a hundred Wrens had been killed in service, including twenty-one en route to Gibraltar for cipher and wireless duties in 1941. Fifteen of them perished when the ship they were on was torpedoed and sunk by a U-boat, and the remaining six lost their lives when the ship that had rescued them from the sea first time round was also torpedoed.

BECOMING PERMANENT

The WRNS was made a permanent part of the Navy after the war in 1945, and by 1949 a long-term career in the Navy became possible for women, although only on land. In 1976, Wrens became subject to the Naval Discipline Act (NDA), which meant amongst other things that they had to march and salute for the first time. Male and female officer training was integrated, as was new-entrant training for ratings in 1981.

GOING TO SEA

Falling Navy recruitment levels in the 1980s caused a rethink about whether women were fit and able to serve at sea – and in 1990 the first female officers and ratings did just that. The WRNS was disbanded altogether in 1993, when women were fully integrated into the Navy and able to serve at all ranks and rates on ships at sea.

THE MODERN NAVY

Today it seems hard to believe that it took so long for women to gain equal opportunities in the Navy when you look at their many achievements since full integration not so long ago.

- ▶ **The first female fighter controller:** Lieutenant Debbie Hitchings was the first woman to become a ship-based fighter controller in the Navy, and she also served on board a submarine for two weeks in 1998 just to prove that it could be done. Her report paved the way for women to join the Submarine Service.

- ▶ **The first female Diving School graduate:** After the Navy decided that women did not after all run a higher risk of decompression sickness than male divers, Lieutenant Catherine Ker became the first female Minewarfare and Clearance Diving Officer in 2010.

▶ **The first female senior observer:** Having joined as a Wren Air Engineering Mechanic in 1988, Lieutenant Commander Kay Burbidge was selected for commission in 1995 and became the FAA's first female senior observer upon joining 829 'Kingfisher' NAS at Culdrose in 2011.

▶ **The first female commanding officer of a major warship:** Having specialised previously in underwater warfare, and with previous commands of Mine Countermeasure Vessels under her belt, Commander Sarah West assumed command of Type 23 frigate HMS *Portland* in 2012.

▶ **The first female Dolphins:** In 2014 three female officers (Lieutenants Maxine Styles, Alexandra Ollson and Penny Thackray) became the first women to earn their 'Dolphin' badges as qualified submariners and went on to serve on Vanguard submarines. All the Navy's submarines are now open to women.

▶ **Woman of the Year:** In 2015, Lieutenant Commander Roxane Heaton was named Woman of the Year at the FDM Everywoman in Technology Awards. The award recognised her achievements at Flag Officer Sea Training HQ, where she developed innovative and cost-effective training solutions that can be used across the Navy and jointly with its allies.

▶ **Rising Star:** 'Junglie' Merlin pilot Lieutenant Natalie Grainger of 846 NAS was given a WATC (WeAreTheCity) Rising Star Award in 2016 after being singled out as a role model for women the world over. Grainger earned her wings in 2011 and flew Sea Kings for the Commando Helicopter Force (CHF) in Afghanistan before returning to play a major part in the smooth transition of CHF to the more modern and powerful Merlins. She also played whenever she could for the Royal Navy Women's Football Team.

▸ **Top employer:** As we have seen, in 2016 the Navy was named one of the top ten British employers in the Workplace Equality Index, quite an achievement just thirteen years after admitting women to the service on an equal footing with men. It was particularly telling that in that same year ninety-seven per cent of working mothers in the Navy chose to return to work after having children.

▸ **The first female Royal Marine Commandos:** From 2019 women will be able to join the Royal Marine Commandos, their one remaining area of exclusion at the time of writing, but of course only those who can get through the commando course at Lympstone will be able to wear the green beret.

ALL IN A DAY'S WORK

Medical Assistant Kate Nesbitt (1988–)

Female officers and ratings have performed a variety of roles and faced equal dangers to the men on the front line since full integration in 1993, including during operations in the Balkans, Iraq and Afghanistan.

In 2009, at the age of just twenty-one, Medical Assistant Kate Nesbitt became the Navy's first woman to be awarded the Military Cross. Attached to 3 Commando Brigade in Afghanistan, she ran 70 metres under fire during a Taliban ambush to administer life-saving aid to a British soldier in the Rifles who had been shot through the mouth and jaw. For the next forty-five minutes she stemmed blood loss and provided the soldier with an alternative airway, all the while subject to gun and rocket fire. The young soldier was eventually airlifted to safety and recovered in time to attend Nesbitt's medal ceremony in Buckingham Palace.

NAVY TRADITIONS

As you might expect from the country's Senior Service, the Navy has many traditions from its long and proud history, from ceremonial dress to the saluting of the quarterdeck, from stone frigates to the invocation of King Neptune when crossing the equator.

UNIFORM

The first uniform appeared for officers in 1748, almost a hundred years after the Royal Navy came into being. The elaborate blue-and-white uniform echoed contemporary fashion, with white breeches and stockings, and was richly decorated with embroidery and gold lace. The dark blue colour used soon became known as 'navy blue', a term that has since been adopted the world over. Epaulettes, peaked caps, frock coats and white helmets and tunics all added to the sense of fashion over the ensuing hundred years or so, and the first version of the current rank insignia, consisting of so many stripes with a curl in the top one, was introduced in 1856.

It wasn't until 1857 that ordinary Jack Tars received a standard uniform for the first time, possibly as a reaction to the captain of the 16-gun brig-sloop HMS *Harlequin* paying for his crews to be dressed as harlequins in the years preceding, there being no regulation to say that he couldn't. Bell-bottomed trousers were to become the most eye-catching element of the ratings' uniform, a look so stylish it was adopted over a hundred years later as one of the iconic items of mainstream fashion in 1970s Britain and America. Since 1997 all male and female ratings have worn the same ceremonial uniform, but the Navy's sense of occasion still requires a few different uniforms to be issued to all officers and ratings.

▶ Blue No. 1 dress: Initially introduced in 1889, this is the formal uniform worn on ceremonial occasions.

▶ Blue No. 2 dress: The mess dress worn for dining in the evening.

▶ Blue No. 3 dress: The practical uniform worn year round for general duties (the white shirt and navy-blue woolly jumper that never seem to leave mainstream fashion belong to No. 3 dress).

▶ Blue No. 4 dress: Previously referred to as 'Action Working Dress' and now officially known as the Royal Navy Personal Clothing System, this 'working in action' uniform was modernised in 2015. More practical, versatile, comfortable and fire-retardant than the previous combat uniform, it has several lightweight layers that are versatile enough to cope with the extremes of climate that the Navy must operate in, from the Arctic to the Gulf.

▶ No. 5 dress: Job-specific working kit that varies according to specialist duties, e.g. as a diver, medical officer or chef, or according to whether you are on board a ship, submarine or aircraft.

▶ White No. 1, 2 and 3 dress: The equivalent of the blue uniforms to be worn in the Tropics.

GETTING TO THE POINT
By 1805 it had been decided that Navy officers needed a light, elaborately decorated dress sword for ceremonial occasions in

addition to the heavier, less decorated fighting sword they needed in battle. There are three dress swords in use today, plus two presentation swords in the Fleet Air Arm.

- ► Royal Navy Officers' Sword: This has a gold-plated brass hilt, white fish-skin grip and brass pommel in the shape of a lion's head, carried within a black rawhide scabbard.

- ► Royal Navy Master at Arms' Sword: Worn by warrant officers today, including the master-at-arms, who is the warrant officer responsible for discipline aboard ship. This sword has a black grip and a rounded pommel.

- ► Royal Marines' Sword: Based on the Infantry Sword of 1897, the blade is finely etched with the crest of the Marines and the grip is made of black sharkskin bound with silver-plated copper wire.

- ► Fleet Air Arm Claymore or Poignard: Both swords are stylised versions of the two-handed Scottish Claymore, with an eagle-winged cross guard. They are presented to mark the achievements of individuals or squadrons.

WHY NAVY OFFICERS CARRY THEIR SWORDS INSTEAD OF WEARING THEM

Because the sword of a Navy officer is traditionally hung from two long straps, as opposed to being hitched to the belt Army-style, officers must support their sword by resting the middle of the scabbard in their hand to prevent it trailing on the ground. The practice probably originated because getting in and out of a boat with a hitched sword was beset with problems.

MEDALS

The first official medals, made of solid gold, were issued in 1794 to the admirals and captains who had fought in the victory over the French at the Battle of the Glorious First of June. The Naval General Service Medal was a campaign medal introduced in 1847 to retrospectively recognise the actions of all ranks in the French Revolutionary, Napoleonic and Anglo-American Wars, and all ratings could hope to one day receive the Long Service and Good Conduct Medal introduced in 1848.

Medals have also been issued, of course, for acts of gallantry, a number of which have been highlighted in earlier chapters of this book. Since 1993, the Conspicuous Gallantry Cross, the Military Cross and the Victoria Cross have been the three gallantry medals that can be awarded to any rank of all three Armed Forces, thereby replacing several medals that were previously available to a single service or to officers or ratings only.

THE NAVY SALUTE

The salute used in the Navy is different to that used in the Army and RAF. The Navy salute takes the shortest route possible by bringing the hand straight up to the side of the head and has the palm turned in, believed to have originated in the days when officers did not want to see the tarred, calloused palms of their ratings when being saluted. The Marines salute in the Army/RAF style, taking the longer route of pushing the hand away from the body before bringing it up to the side of the head with the palm facing out for all to see.

NAVAL ENSIGNS

An ensign is a naval flag used to denote the nationality of a vessel, flown from the stern while in port and either from the stern or a more central position when underway. A national flag is flown as a 'jack' on the bow, but normally only when a vessel is in port or at anchor.

The White Ensign, which is a red St George's Cross on a white background and a Union Flag in the canton (the upper corner next to the flagstaff), is flown by the British Navy on all its vessels and shore establishments, including those of the Royal Marines. By special dispensation, it can also be flown by yachts belonging to members of the prestigious Royal Yacht Squadron on the Isle of Wight.

The Red Ensign is flown by the Merchant Navy and the Blue Ensign can be flown on British merchant ships commanded by a Royal Naval Reserve officer, or whose officers and crew include enough RN reservists or retirees to warrant the flag. The Blue Ensign is also flown by the ships of the Royal Fleet Auxiliary, Royal Research Ships and British-registered yachts belonging to yacht clubs with the necessary warrant in the UK, Australia and New Zealand, including the Royal Naval Sailing Association.

FLYING THE FLAG ACROSS THE POND

The US Navy destroyer USS *Winston S. Churchill* has a Royal Navy officer, usually a Navigation Officer, permanently assigned to her. For that reason, she also flies the White Ensign on her port yardarm on ceremonial occasions. These naval honours reflect the wartime achievements of the British prime minister (and it may have done no harm that Churchill's mother was American).

TRAFALGAR DAY

Trafalgar Day is celebrated around Britain and beyond each year on 21 October, the date of the battle in 1805. A ceremony is held at the oldest statue of Lord Nelson, which is in Birmingham, and the flag signal 'England expects that every man will do his duty' is flown from the Nelson Monument in Edinburgh. A service is held at Trafalgar Cemetery in Gibraltar, where some sailors later died of the wounds they had received during the battle, and an annual festival is held in the small town of Trafalgar in Victoria, New South Wales.

The commissioned officers of the Royal Navy and other Commonwealth navies finish the day with a Trafalgar Night dinner and the traditional toast to Lord Nelson, 'The Immortal Memory'.

PICKLE NIGHT

Around 4 November each year, the celebration of Pickle Night is held by the Navy's warrant officers and senior ratings, HMS *Pickle* being the schooner that arrived in Falmouth on 4 November 1805 to deliver news of victory at the Battle of Trafalgar. The *Pickle* sank after running aground off Cadiz in 1808, but a replica was built in 1995 and is now a museum ship in Kingston-upon-Hull Marina, from where she also makes frequent voyages.

CROSSING THE LINE

The Crossing the Line ceremony is enacted whenever a Navy ship crosses the equator, being considered necessary to pay due respect to His Oceanic Majesty, King Neptune. Once Neptune and the members of his court, aka certain senior ratings of the ship's company, have meted out justice on various trumped-up charges, all novice officers and ratings – and anyone else picked on by Neptune's court – are initiated into the Brotherhood of the Sea. Having been lathered with shaving cream or mashed potato, they are mock-shaved with a huge cut-throat razor and tipped backwards into a tank of water.

NAVY SPEAK
PUTTING THE QUEEN TO BED

This delightful piece of Navy speak refers to the evening colours ceremony, which involves lowering a ship's ensign and jack at sunset.

'HEART OF OAK'

The traditional quick march of the Navy is 'Heart of Oak', a naval march composed by William Boyce in the eighteenth century. The patriotic lyrics that go with it were written by English actor David Garrick to commemorate British military victories abroad in 1759, including the sea battles at Lagos and Quiberon Bay. The chorus goes as follows:

Heart of Oak are our ships
Jolly Tars are our men
We always are ready: Steady, boys, Steady!
We'll fight and we'll conquer again and again.

The rhythm of the song was subsequently used by the Navy's drummers when beating to quarters (clearing the gun decks of a sailing ship for action). 'Heart of Oak' refers to the strongest pieces of wood from the middle of the oak tree, the primary material for the building of warships at that time.

'A LIFE ON THE OCEAN WAVE'

The Regimental Quick March of the Marines is 'A Life on the Ocean Wave', a song written by Henry Russell in 1838 and arranged for the Marines in 1882. The RM Commandos March is 'Sarie Marais', originally the tune of a song popular with the impressive Boer commandos who fought the British in South Africa.

ENTERING OR LEAVING HARBOUR

There are three procedures for a Navy warship or submarine entering or leaving harbour: Alpha, Bravo and Charlie. Procedure Charlie is the routine method, without ceremonials. Procedure Bravo requires all personnel to line up along the upper deck (or on top of the submarine) in their everyday No. 3 dress. Procedure Alpha requires all personnel to line up in ceremonial No. 1 dress, often used to celebrate a vessel's return to a friendly port after months away on operations or the arrival of a Navy ship on a goodwill visit abroad.

STONE FRIGATES

The tradition of referring to Navy shore establishments as 'stone frigates' and naming them 'HMS something or other' as if they were real ships has its origins in the Battle of Diamond Rock in 1805, when Lieutenant James Wilkes Maurice was commanded to man the eponymous lump of rock off Martinique with 120 men and cannons taken ashore from his ship. Because he successfully harassed French warships from this position for a while, the rock became known as a 'sloop of war' like any other.

Until the late nineteenth century the Navy housed training and other support facilities in decommissioned ships moored in ports. The ships retained their original names and when their facilities finally moved ashore to enjoy more modern facilities they took their names with them, partly because until 1959 only officers and ratings who were listed as serving on 'ships of war' were subject to the Naval Discipline Act. Two of the earliest stone frigates (somewhere along the line, 'sloop of war perched on a rock' had been modernised to 'stone frigate') were the engineering training college HMS Marlborough, which moved ashore to Portsmouth in 1880, and the gunnery training school HMS Excellent, which moved ashore to Whale Island in 1891.

One of the great traditions of the Navy that prevails to this day is that you 'go on board' when you enter a stone frigate and 'go ashore' when you leave it.

SALUTING THE QUARTERDECK

On crossing in either direction over the brow, the gangplank that links a ship to shore, all RN and RM personnel pause to salute the quarterdeck. The quarterdeck, which is effectively the rear of a ship today, remains the spiritual heart of a ship, taking its name from the physical quarterdeck that was built at the stern of the sailing warships of yesteryear, where a religious shrine would have been set up. The quarterdeck was the highest point of the ship and was so called because it was a quarter of the size of all the other decks below it (visit HMS *Victory* at Portsmouth Historic Dockyard if you want to stand on the one on which Nelson fell while commanding the Battle of Trafalgar).

Many stone frigates have areas decorated like shipboard quarterdecks to allow the tradition of saluting the quarterdeck to take place in time-honoured fashion.

TOASTS

As you might expect from a fighting force that once part-paid its sailors with rum or beer, a few drinking toasts have become traditional along the way.

The Loyal Toast is made each evening to the monarch, spoken by the youngest officer present at the mess dinner. This toast is generally made sitting down, a tradition that is said to have been initiated by Charles II and/or William IV after they bumped their head on a ship's beam when they rose to reply in person to the Loyal Toast on board.

The youngest officer then delivers the Daily Toast from the set of standard toasts that have been handed down through the centuries:

- ▶ Monday: 'Our ships at sea'

- ▶ Tuesday: 'Our men'

- ▶ Wednesday: 'Ourselves'

- ▶ Thursday: 'A bloody war or a sickly season'

- ▶ Friday: 'A willing foe and sea-room'

- ▶ Saturday: 'Sweethearts and wives (may they never meet)'

- ▶ Sunday: 'Absent friends'

Notes:

Although 'Our men' and 'Sweethearts and wives' are still widely used, they were officially changed in 2013 to reflect the fact that women had already been serving at sea for almost two decades. The toasts are now officially 'Our sailors' and 'Our families' respectively, but tradition remains stronger in most messes.

The Thursday toast originally reflected the fact that promotions were likely to come much more quickly at times of war or general sickness – at one time it probably felt like all you had to do to secure promotion was to not catch scurvy.

Manners and etiquette are strictly adhered to at mess dinners. The mess silver must not be touched until after the Loyal Toast, the port is always passed to the left without the decanter leaving the table top and elbows are not allowed to touch the table – although an exception to this latter rule may be made for sailors who have rounded Cape Horn and/or the Cape of Good Hope, at the rate of one elbow per cape.

ROYAL YACHTS

It was a long-standing tradition for the Navy to provide the Royal Yachtsmen, from the vessel's captain to the stewards. The Marines provided protection whenever the Royal Family were on board, and the Royal Marines Band Service provided the music on special or ceremonial occasions.

The first royal yacht was HMY *Mary*, a gift from the Dutch in 1660 to celebrate the restoration of the British monarchy under Charles II. Most of the eighty-five royal yachts were purpose built, although some were commandeered from the Royal or Merchant Navy. The last Royal Navy vessel to be commandeered (for the 1947 Royal Tour of South Africa) was HMS *Vanguard*, the last battleship to be built anywhere in the world.

In 1997 the last royal yacht, HMY *Britannia*, was decommissioned and now serves as a visitor attraction in Leith, Edinburgh. During forty-three years of service she travelled over one million nautical miles around the globe, flying the flag and drumming up business for

Britain on 696 foreign visits. From the honeymoon cruise of Prince Charles and Princess Diana to the evacuation of over a thousand refugees from civil war in Aden, she had many varied visitors on board, including four US presidents (Eisenhower, Ford, Reagan and Clinton). Her final foreign engagement was to bring home the last Governor of Hong Kong, Chris Patten, after that territory had been handed back to the Chinese in 1997. She was also designated the ship on which the Queen and immediate members of the Royal Family would have taken refuge in the event of a nuclear incident during the Cold War.

NAVY SPEAK
KNOCK SEVEN BELLS OUT OF SOMEONE

Because eight bells signify the end of a watch, knocking seven bells out of someone means to give them a good hiding and yet stop short of finishing them off.

The only time that eight bells can be bettered is when sixteen bells are rung at midnight on New Year's Eve: eight to see out the old year and eight to bring in the new.

FIGUREHEADS AND BADGES

Since earliest times, people decorated the bows of their wooden warships to make them look fierce or to ward off evil spirits and sea monsters. The Royal Navy used huge carved figureheads on the bow to signify a vessel's importance and to help those who could not read (or who could not read English, at least) know which ship it was. The figurehead was always in keeping with the ship's name, such that HMS *Glasgow*, for example, had a figurehead depicting a Scottish soldier in a kilt. The iron-hulled HMS *Warrior* and *Black Prince* were the last British battleships to carry huge figureheads on their bows.

Even when ships began to be built of metal, the custom of decorating them continued. Badges were displayed around the ship and smaller versions were mounted on wooden 'honours boards' displaying the ship's battle honours, a tradition that continues to this day. Guns have special plugs known as tompions to keep out rain and sea spray and these too have been decorated with a badge reflecting the ship's name.

Although they were previously different shapes to match the size of ship, round badges are now assigned to all RN ships, submarines and air squadrons, with shore establishments being assigned badges which are an offset square in shape. Each badge has the Navy crown sitting on top and gold-coloured rope running around the outside. Royal Marine units have their own badges, usually in the shape of a shield and without the Navy crown and gold-coloured rope.

BATTLE HONOURS

The honours displayed on battle boards on ships and submarines are the Navy equivalent of the battles displayed on the regimental colours within the Army. The honours are awarded to individual ships but are also included in a cumulative record of all vessels that have borne the same name over the long history of the Navy. HMS *Warspite* has more cumulative battle honours than any other British warship (twenty-five), and the Queen Elizabeth-class battleship *Warspite* launched in 1913 has the most battle honours ever awarded to an individual ship in the Navy (seventeen), which are as follows:

World War One
  ► Jutland 1916

World War Two
  ► Atlantic 1939

  ► Narvik 1940

- ► Norway 1940

- ► Calabria 1940

- ► Mediterranean 1940, 1941, 1943

- ► Malta Convoys 1941

- ► Cape Matapan 1941

- ► Crete 1941

- ► Sicily 1943

- ► Salerno 1943

- ► English Channel 1944

- ► Normandy 1944

- ► Biscay 1944

- ► Walcheren 1944

NAVY SPORTS

Competitive sport and high levels of fitness are very much in keeping with the ethos of the Royal Navy and Marines, which means that sport is actively encouraged at every level. There are seventy-one sports associations and clubs in the Naval Service and the wide range of sports enjoyed include football, rugby, judo, fencing, gymnastics, weightlifting, athletics, netball, archery, cycling, volleyball, bobsleigh, skiing, snowboarding, showjumping, boxing and, of course, swimming, rowing and sailing. In other words: you name it, the Navy plays it.

As you might expect, there is a degree of rivalry between teams from different units, squadrons, arms and services, some of which have long since captured the public imagination, like the Navy v. Army rugby match that sells out Twickenham every year. There are a great many interservice competitions across a range of summer and winter sports, often including separate women's and seniors' events.

The Navy v. Army Rugby Match

First played in 1907 just after the Navy and Army Rugby Unions had been formed, the Centenary Match was held in 2017 (it took 110 years to complete the centenary because the world wars twice stopped play). The Navy won that first match in 1907, but there is no real need to mention here which team is way ahead in overall victories (it's not the Navy, I'm afraid). One of the most thrilling matches ever was the 29–29 draw in 2016 after the Navy fought back from a deficit of 26–7. Since 1920, when the RAF Rugby Union was formed, the match has been played as part of the tripartite Interservices Championship.

The Royal Naval Sailing Association (RNSA)

Founded in 1935, the RNSA has over 5,000 members and more than 200 events in their calendar each year. It is the largest sailing association in the UK, providing the means for serving and retired sailors of all ranks and rates to enjoy racing and recreational sailing in all its forms, including offshore and inshore yacht racing, powerboating, cruising, dinghies and windsurfing. It also organised and ran the first ever Whitbread Round the World Yacht Race (now the Volvo Ocean Race) in 1973, using the Portsmouth Naval Base as its starting line.

The Royal Navy and Royal Marines Charity Field Gun Competition

Competed for annually at HMS Collingwood in Fareham, the Brickwoods Trophy is a contest to see who can transport a field gun and its associated equipment over an obstacle course in the shortest time. The competition had its origins in the Relief of Ladysmith during the Second Boer War, when the Naval Brigade took heavy naval guns ashore and hauled them over difficult terrain to assist in the land battle. Today, each crew of eighteen field gunners assemble an antique field gun and run with it, disassembling and reassembling it as the competition requires, before dragging it home. The trophy was provided by Brickwoods Brewery, the original sponsor of the competition, in 1907 and is a silver replica of a 12-pounder field gun and its sailor crew of seven.

The first winners of the competition in 1907 were a Royal Marines Light Infantry gun crew. At the time of writing, the record time of 1 minute 18.88 seconds was set by HMS Collingwood in 2001.

The Gibraltar Rock Race

It is a tradition for a ship's company visiting Gibraltar to take on the famous Rock Race at dawn. The route involves a 2.7-mile run up to the summit of the rock, a strenuous 1,300-foot climb with gradients of up to 1:4. The current record of 17 minutes 29 seconds was set in 1986 by then Sub Lieutenant Chris Robison, who was stopped off with HMS *Glasgow* en route to a Mediterranean deployment. Over 40,000 people have run the race since, but no one has come close to that record. In defence of the other 40,000 people, though, Robison was once the Scottish cross-country champion.

The United States Marine Corps Challenge Trophy (Tunney Cup)

The Challenge Trophy is an annual football competition involving teams from different RM units over one week at the Commando Training Centre. The magnificent cup they play for was presented in 1928 by Captain Gene Tunney of the US Marines Corps, who happened to be the world heavyweight boxing champion at the time. This was a goodwill gesture after the Royal Marines had presented the US Marines with a British bulldog called Private Pagett.

The World Champion skier

Submariner Brett Wild took time off from serving on board HMS *Ambush* in 2017 to lead Paralympic skier Millie Knight to gold medal success in the World Para Alpine Skiing Championships in the Italian Alps. Millie had lost most of her vision by the age of six, but having a sighted guide allows her to compete at the highest levels of international competition.

THE BEIRA BUCKET

One less glamorous but nonetheless prestigious sporting trophy competed for between 1966 and 1975 was the Beira Bucket. The many ships involved in the blockade of Rhodesia through the port of Beira in Mozambique relieved their boredom by competing in inter-ship sporting competitions for an old, bashed metal bucket, which became 'decorated' over the years by its various holders, who each painted an illustration of their ship's name on it.

THE SERIOUS BUSINESS OF PERFORMANCE REPORTING

Serving in the Navy is a serious business, so a sense of humour has always been required to maintain some equilibrium. In the era that preceded political correctness, that sense of humour found its way into the system used to report on an officer's performance and potential. Here is just a sample of the masterful ways in which bitter pills were sweetened for those on the receiving end of some of those reports:

'I WOULD NOT BREED FROM THIS OFFICER.'

'HE HAS CARRIED OUT EACH AND EVERY ONE OF HIS DUTIES TO HIS ENTIRE SATISFACTION.'

'HE WOULD BE OUT OF HIS DEPTH IN A CAR PARK PUDDLE.'

'THIS YOUNG LADY HAS DELUSIONS OF ADEQUACY.'

'THIS MEDICAL OFFICER HAS USED MY SHIP TO CARRY HIS GENITALS FROM PORT TO PORT, AND MY OFFICERS TO CARRY HIM FROM BAR TO BAR.'

'HE HAS THE WISDOM OF YOUTH AND THE ENERGY OF OLD AGE.'

'THIS OFFICER SHOULD GO FAR – AND THE SOONER HE STARTS, THE BETTER.'

'IN MY OPINION THIS PILOT SHOULD NOT BE ALLOWED TO FLY BELOW 250 FEET.'

'HE DONATED HIS BODY TO SCIENCE BEFORE HE WAS DONE USING IT.'

KEEPING THE WORLD INFORMED

The Navy today does a fine job on keeping the world informed about what it is doing, with two million followers on Twitter alongside its traditional paper publications.

- *Navy News:* The monthly colour newspaper of the Navy since 1954, read by officers and ratings alike, and by anyone else who is interested in all things Navy. Contains news about the Navy's people, including the Marines, and about current events and the activities of ships, submarines and aircraft within the fleet. There are also book reviews, letters, news about reunions and the latest Navy sporting news, plus Tuggs' cartoon strips about the life and times of Jack, Jenny and Royal. Around 35,000 copies are printed monthly and the web version is updated every weekday of the year.

- *The Globe and Laurel:* The official journal of the Marines since 1892. Published six times a year, it is essential reading for members of the corps past and present, and anyone else interested in keeping up with the latest news on the Royal Marines. It contains reports from all major units, ships' detachments, the Reserves and the Cadets. In line with *Navy News*, it provides book reviews, letters, news about reunions and the latest RM sporting news. It is put together at Royal Marines HQ at Whale Island in Portsmouth and 12,500 copies of each edition are distributed around the world.

- *The Maritime Reservist:* The twice-yearly magazine for Royal Naval and Royal Marines Reservists, including news about their involvement in operations and exercises at home and abroad.

- *The Blue Band:* The journal of the Royal Marines Band Service and Royal Naval Volunteer Bands, containing the latest news and details of concerts and displays. It is distributed worldwide three times a year.

THE NAVY IN POPULAR CULTURE

The Navy has exerted a huge influence on popular culture since its beginnings as a permanent force in the seventeenth century, inspiring art and literature, musical compositions, films and TV programmes galore. Over a thousand books and more than twenty films and TV programmes have been produced on Horatio Nelson alone.

The Navy is not averse to providing its own popular culture either. The Sods Opera is the long-standing tradition of a ship's company providing its own morale-boosting entertainment at sea (Sods being an acronym of Ship's Operatic and Drama Society), while back on dry land there is a thriving Royal Navy Theatre Association (RNTA). The RNTA runs an annual festival and awards ceremony in Portsmouth, attended by local Navy theatre clubs from around the country.

MUSIC

Since the early days of drumming, playing the fife and singing sea shanties like 'What Shall We Do with the Drunken Sailor?' (reportedly popular during hull-cleaning duties), the Navy has been inspiring nautical-themed music and song, from operatic to pop and everything in between.

THE LAST NIGHT OF THE PROMS
Britain's proud naval history is celebrated in the Royal Albert Hall each year, as the concluding session of the entire Proms season has for many years included a hearty rendition of 'Fantasia on British Sea Songs', the nine-part medley composed by Henry Wood in 1905 to commemorate the centenary of the Battle of Trafalgar. Even in the years when the entire Fantasia has not been performed, the ninth and final part, 'Rule, Britannia!', has been retained in its own right.

HMS PINAFORE
First performed in 1878, *HMS Pinafore* is one of Gilbert and Sullivan's most enduring comic operas. It tells the story of a Navy captain's daughter falling in love with an ordinary sailor when her father has plans to marry her to the First Lord of the Admiralty. This was the cue for a lampooning of the class system of the time within British society – and the Navy in particular.

'SAILING'
Rod Stewart's biggest UK hit single was 'Sailing', a release from his 1975 *Atlantic Crossing* album. In 1976, it was used as the opening theme of the BBC documentary series *Sailor* about the Western Atlantic deployment of the aircraft carrier HMS *Ark Royal*, and a 1977 version by the Ship's Company and Royal Marines Band of HMS *Ark Royal* also went platinum. In 1982, the Rod Stewart version was played from the tannoys on Portsmouth Harbour as the British task force set off for the Falkland Islands.

THE MILITARY WIVES CHOIRS
The choir formed by Gareth Malone for the 2011 BBC series *The Choir: Military Wives* was formed of the wives and girlfriends of the Commando Logistics Regiment of RMB Chivenor, then serving in Afghanistan. Along with a second choir formed at the Royal Citadel in

Plymouth, home to three gunner batteries of 29 Commando Regiment Royal Artillery, a single was released and shot to fame as that year's Christmas number one single 'Wherever You Are'. The first album followed in 2012, by then including the choirs of Commando Training Centre, Lympstone, HMNB Portsmouth and the Scots Guards in Catterick (who had in fact contacted Gareth Malone in the first place, after forming their own choir in 2010). The runaway success story continues, with huge sums being raised for military charities as a result.

LITERATURE, FILM AND TV

In addition to the great naval histories written over the last century by the likes of Arthur J. Marder, David and Stephen Howarth, Tom Pocock, Peter Padfield and N. A. M. Rodger, British writers have also produced great fictional stories centred around our naval heroes and their exploits at sea, many of which have proved irresistible to film and TV producers. Reality TV has also found its way into the Navy and Marines in recent years.

HORATIO HORNBLOWER

Set in the age of Nelson, C. S. Forester's ten Horatio Hornblower novels appeared between 1937 and 1962. Their combination of brilliant battle descriptions and courageous but self-doubting hero lent themselves perfectly to the screen, resulting in the 1951 film *Captain Horatio Hornblower*, starring Gregory Peck, and a British TV series of eight episodes between 1998 and 2003, called *Hornblower* and starring Ioan Gruffudd.

THE BOUNTY

Of all the five films made about the mutiny on the Bounty, the 1984 version, *The Bounty*, starring Anthony Hopkins as Captain Bligh and Mel Gibson as Fletcher Christian, is considered the most historically accurate. Charles Laughton and Trevor Howard are other notable names to have played Captain Bligh, while Errol Flynn, Clark Gable and Marlon Brando are the other big names to have enjoyed the role of Fletcher Christian.

THE CRUEL SEA

World War Two convoy duty in the North Atlantic was evocatively portrayed in the 1951 novel *The Cruel Sea*, based on the author Nicholas Monsarrat's own experience of service. In the 1953 film version of the book, the narrator, Lieutenant Commander George Ericson, was played by Jack Hawkins.

HMS DEFIANT

Another story of naval rebellion, this time the Spithead Mutiny of 1797, was told in the 1962 film *HMS Defiant*, starring Alec Guinness and Dirk Bogarde. The screenplay was based on Frank Tilsley's 1958 novel *Mutiny*.

SINK THE BISMARCK!

Another British book turned film was the 1959 C. S. Forester novel *The Last Nine Days of the Bismarck*, the story about the greatest sea hunt of all time. It was turned into the 1960 critically acclaimed film *Sink the Bismarck!* starring Kenneth More.

PATRICK O'BRIAN'S NOVELS

The twenty acclaimed novels of Patrick O'Brian, published between 1969 and 1999, were set during the Napoleonic Wars and were meticulous reconstructions of the age of fighting sail. They began with *Master and Commander* in 1969, which was turned into the 2003 film *Master and Commander: The Far Side of the World*, starring Russell Crowe and Paul Bettany. The books follow the adventures of Captain Jack Aubrey and his ship's surgeon, Stephen Maturin, who enjoy an 'opposites attract' relationship.

IAN FLEMING AND 007

During World War Two, author Ian Fleming was a Naval Intelligence Officer and would therefore have been aware that all classified documents were coded '00' and that '007' was the particular code assigned to the breaking of the German diplomatic code. It may have been a coincidence that he gave his fictional secret agent James

Bond the code name 007, but it doesn't take a cryptanalyst to figure out that it probably wasn't.

REALITY TV

The twenty-first-century obsession with watching real people do real things on TV has included the following programmes on the Navy and Marines.

- ► *Building Britain's Ultimate Warship* (Channel 4, 2010): A documentary on the construction, launch and testing of the destroyer HMS *Daring*.

- ► *Royal Marines Commando School* (Channel 4, 2014): A series that allowed us to watch marines suffer and ultimately fail or triumph over the commando course at Lympstone.

- ► *Royal Navy School* (Channel 4, 2016): A series that followed the gruelling basic training of recruits trying to join the Navy at HMS Raleigh.

- ► *Devonport: Inside the Royal Navy* (Quest, 2016): A fly-on-the-wall documentary about the naval base and those who work there.

- ► *Warship* (Channel 4, 2017): A documentary on board the assault ship HMS *Ocean* as she sailed to the Persian Gulf to take command of an international task force there.

ART

Countless pictures of naval battles, vessels and heroes have been painted since the very early days of the fighting age of sail. The collection on display at the National Museum of the Royal Navy in Portsmouth is in itself impressive, housing one of the most important collections of Nelson portraits anywhere. Many great British artists have captured naval vessels or battles on canvas, but arguably none have done so better than Nicholas Pocock, J. M. W. Turner and W. L. Wyllie.

NICHOLAS POCOCK (1740-1821)

Known for his many detailed paintings of naval battles, including his bird's-eye view of the 1801 Battle of Copenhagen. He took his work so seriously that he was present at the Battle of the Glorious First of June in 1794 on board the frigate HMS *Pegasus*.

J. M. W. TURNER (1775-1851)

Not many artists could capture a sea scene like Turner. His renowned painting *The Fighting Temeraire* evocatively depicts that warship being towed up the Thames to be broken up after a long and distinguished career, including having fought at Trafalgar – at one point with an enemy ship on either side of her.

W. L. WYLLIE (1851-1931)

Wyllie's vast *The Panorama of the Battle of Trafalgar* was painted in 1929 in situ at the Museum of the Royal Navy in Portsmouth. Measuring 42 x 12 feet (12.8 x 3.7 metres), it took Wyllie over nine months at the age of seventy-nine to complete it, often painting on ladders to reach the top half of the canvas.

NAVAL MUSEUMS AND WAR MEMORIALS

With several hundred years of naval history to celebrate, it comes as no surprise that a fair bit of museum space is needed to house the exhibits, especially as some of those exhibits are warships from across the ages. Portsmouth Historic Dockyard and its surrounding area provide most of that space, while a good chunk of RNAS Yeovilton has been given over to house the Fleet Air Arm Museum.

A great many sacrifices have been made, so it is fitting that impressive memorials exist to commemorate them, especially when so many of those who lost their lives have no graves but the sea.

NAVAL MUSEUMS AND HISTORIC SHIPS

PORTSMOUTH HISTORIC DOCKYARD

Portsmouth Historic Dockyard sits alongside HMNB Portsmouth and contains the National Museum of the Royal Navy as well as the following historic ships.

▶ *Mary Rose*: Henry VIII's flagship, along with the astonishing collection of artefacts recovered from the sea when the vessel was raised in 1982.

▶ HMS *Victory*: Lord Nelson's flagship at the Battle of Trafalgar looks as impressive today as she did on that victorious yet fateful day in 1805.

▶ HMS *Warrior* 1860: The warship that made the transition from sail to steam, she looks every inch the hybrid she was as the world's first iron-hulled, steam-powered warship but still with a broadside gun arrangement and three masts to carry the sails that supplemented her steam power.

▶ HMS *M.33*: The sole survivor of the Dardanelles Campaign of 1915–16 and one of just three British warships from World War One still in existence.

THE ROYAL NAVY SUBMARINE MUSEUM, GOSPORT

Reachable by complimentary water bus from Portsmouth Historic Dockyard, the Submarine Museum includes the following vessels.

▶ *Holland 1*: The Navy's first ever submarine, launched in 1901.

▶ *X24*: A World War Two midget submarine.

▶ HMS *Alliance*: An ocean-going submarine built during World War Two and serving through much of the Cold War era.

DEVONPORT NAVAL HERITAGE CENTRE

Open for special events and advance bookings, the Naval Heritage Centre at Devonport explains the history of the vast naval dockyard there and some of the ships that have sailed from it over the last 300 years, including the on-site HMS *Courageous*, the only nuclear submarine open to the public anywhere. It also has some important collections of naval dress, swords, figureheads, ship models and memorabilia.

EXPLOSION! THE MUSEUM OF NAVAL FIREPOWER, GOSPORT

Also reachable by complimentary water bus from Portsmouth Historic Dockyard, the former armament depot at Priddy's Hard tells the story of naval firepower through the ages, beginning with the gunpowder produced at the time of Nelson's Navy. Exhibits include naval guns, mines, depth charges, torpedoes, cruise missiles and nuclear bombs.

THE ROYAL MARINES MUSEUM

The proud 350-year history of the elite fighting force was until recently displayed in their museum on Eastney Esplanade in Southsea, instantly recognisable by the impressive 'Yomper' statue out front on the esplanade. It has now closed but its state-of-the-art replacement will open in 2020 at Portsmouth Historic Dockyard.

THE FLEET AIR ARM MUSEUM, YEOVILTON

Housed at RNAS Yeovilton, the Fleet Air Arm Museum opened with just eight aircraft in 1964, the fiftieth anniversary year of the FAA (or Royal Naval Air Service as it was then). Now the largest naval aviation museum in Europe and the second largest worldwide, it has over ninety aircraft on display, from a Sopwith Baby biplane from World War One to one of the Sea King helicopters that has served the FAA so well for thirty-five years. There is also a Concorde and an award-winning experience replicating life on board the aircraft carrier HMS *Ark Royal*.

HMS *CAROLINE*, BELFAST

The light cruiser HMS *Caroline*, now a museum ship in the Alexandra Dock of the Titanic Quarter in Belfast, is today the sole survivor from the Battle of Jutland.

HMS *TRINCOMALEE*, HARTLEPOOL

The oldest warship in the world still afloat is HMS *Trincomalee*, berthed at Jackson Dock in Hartlepool. Launched in Bombay in 1817, she was a light, speedy frigate that concentrated her firepower on one deck.

HMS *BELFAST*, LONDON

Sitting just upstream from Tower Bridge, the light cruiser HMS *Belfast* belongs to the Imperial War Museum. Launched in 1938, she spent two years protecting the Arctic Convoys, and on D-Day she fired some of the first shots that provided cover for the landings.

NAVY WAR MEMORIALS

There is no headstone among the flowers for those who perish at sea.

REAR ADMIRAL PHILIP WILCOCKS

THE NAVAL MEMORIALS AT PORTSMOUTH, PLYMOUTH AND CHATHAM

After World War One, the Admiralty decided that three identical giant obelisks should be erected at the Navy's three 'manning ports' of Portsmouth, Plymouth and Chatham to commemorate the sailors who lost their lives during the war. Following World War Two, it was decided to extend each of the monuments outwards at ground level to add the names of those who had lost their lives during that conflict. The Portsmouth monument stands proud on

Southsea Common; the Plymouth one on the Hoe overlooking Plymouth Sound; and the Chatham one overlooks the town from a nearby hill.

THE ROYAL NAVAL DIVISION MEMORIAL
The Royal Naval Division Memorial is situated outside the Old Admiralty Building on Horse Guards Parade in London to commemorate the members of the division who died during World War One. Other RND memorials stand in France, at Beaucourt near the Somme (the Battle of the Ancre) and at Gavrelle (the Battle of Arras).

THE ROYAL MARINES MEMORIAL
Rededicated in 2000 as the national monument of the Marines, the bronze sculpture on the Mall near Admiralty Arch was originally erected in 1903 in memory of fallen marines in the Boxer Rebellion and Second Boer War.

THE COMMANDO MEMORIAL
The Commando Memorial at Spean Bridge in Scotland overlooks the training depot set up to train all commandos during World War Two, including, therefore, those of the nine RM Commando battalions. The impressive bronze sculpture features three commandos looking towards Ben Nevis in the Scottish Highlands.

THE YOMPER STATUE
Unveiled by Margaret Thatcher in 1992, the Yomper statue depicting a marine during the Falklands Conflict stands in front of the old Royal Marines Museum at Eastney.

WOODLANDS GARDEN,
45 COMMANDO, RM CONDOR
This garden of remembrance is a living monument to the fallen of 45 Commando since the unit moved to Arbroath in 1971. It is unique in that it includes substantial rocks from each of the places

in the world where their members have fallen: Northern Ireland, the Falklands, Kosovo, Iraq and Afghanistan.

THE NATIONAL SUBMARINE WAR MEMORIAL
The National Submarine War Memorial is set into the wall of Victoria Embankment in London as a memorial to all the submariners who died in the world wars.

THE FLEET AIR ARM MEMORIALS
A number of FAA memorials exist to remember some or all of those who have lost their lives in the service.

- ► Victoria Embankment: Erected outside the MoD building in Victoria Embankment Gardens in memory of all those who have lost their lives serving in the RNAS and FAA.

- ► Lee-on-Solent: Erected on the site of a large naval air station during World War Two to commemorate the 1,925 members of the FAA who have no known grave from that conflict.

- ► RNAS Culdrose: To commemorate the loss of seven members of 849 NAS in Iraq in 2003.

- ► Ramsgate, Dover Harbour and the Spitfire Museum in Manston: Three memorials to the Channel Dash in 1942.

- ► Borneo: The Junglie Memorial at Nanga Gaat to remember the sixteen helicopter crew who lost their lives on Borneo in the 1960s.

THE RFA MEMORIAL, MARCHWOOD, HAMPSHIRE
This memorial remembers those who lost their lives on board RFA *Sir Galahad* and RFA *Sir Tristram* during the Falklands Conflict and

is made partly from carved rock brought from East Falkland. There is also a memorial to those same men on East Falkland itself.

THE NATIONAL MEMORIAL ARBORETUM

The National Memorial Arboretum near Lichfield in Staffordshire was created in 2001 and holds around 300 memorials, including the Naval Service Memorial and other memorials dedicated to individual branches and ships of the Navy as well as the other four arms of the Naval Service (the FAA, Royal Marines, Submarine Service and RFA).

NAVAL SERVICE CHARITIES AND ASSOCIATIONS

Many thriving groups exist to represent the different branches of the Naval Service and several charities exist to provide help to those in need.

THE ROYAL NAVY AND ROYAL MARINES CHARITY (RNRMC)

Run from an office on Whale Island since its inception in 2007, the Royal Navy and Royal Marines Charity exists to support personnel and their families for life. It raises millions of pounds each year, with £45 million raised in its first ten years of existence. The funds are used to support worthy causes just about anywhere the Navy has a presence around the world. Four specific charities come under the umbrella of the RNRMC: the Royal Naval Officers' Charity, the Naval Service Sports Charity, the Royal Marines Charity and the Royal Marines Sports Association.

TOT FUND

After the rum ration had been withdrawn from the Navy on Black Tot Day, 31 July 1970, the American businessman Charles Tobias secured the right to make Pusser's Rum using the original Navy Rum formula. It was a requirement, though, that the sale of each bottle would result in a royalty payment to the RNRMC. These royalties are known as the Tot Fund, and there is wording on the label of each bottle that explains this arrangement to buyers of the product. Tens of thousands of pounds are raised in this way each year. Please drink more Pusser's Rum.

THE ROYAL NAVAL ASSOCIATION (RNA)

There are 370 like-minded branches of the RNA around the country, with over 20,000 members in total. Each branch hosts regular social events, advises on welfare matters and undertakes fundraising activities. All current and former Naval Service personnel, relatives and supporters are welcome to join.

THE ROYAL MARINES ASSOCIATION (RMA)

The RMA exists to offer support, stability and friendship to the Royal Marines family, including cadets, recruits, serving personnel and veterans. Branches around the country arrange local social and fundraising events, but come together at Lympstone for the Annual Corps Family Weekend.

Fundraising events throughout the UK include pantomimes put on by serving and retired marines. Appearances of the Corps de Ballet are a highlight, when marines in ballerina costume and Army boots deliver their routine with a comic lack of grace and timing guaranteed to raise money for RMA causes.